PRAISE FO
THE DUDE'S GUIDE TO MARRIAGE

"My friend Darrin Patrick has written an excellent book to help men develop the skills needed to love and serve their wives well. It is full of wisdom, honesty, and is extremely practical. *The Dude's Guide to Marriage* provides for us a beautiful real-life picture of what a marriage centered on the gospel looks like amid the daily grind of life."

—Matt Chandler, lead pastor of The Village Church, president of Acts 29 Church Planting Network, and author of *The Mingling of Souls*

"In this book, Darrin and Amie Patrick give us down-to-earth, practical words of wisdom to young men about relating to their wives well. This book is solidly biblical, gospel rich, and helpfully practical. The Patricks don't deal in airy abstractions but give concrete guidance for men about what it takes to succeed as husbands. *The Dude's Guide to Marriage* is brimming with valuable insight gained from years of experience. It would be a great book to give to a couple in premarital counseling or to share with a long-time married couple, still learning, as we all are, how to grow together in Christ. I highly recommend it."

—Russell Moore, president of Southern Baptist Ethics and Religious Liberty Commission

"My wife, Pam, and I have benefitted from Darrin and Amie Patrick's personal wisdom and example the past few years. Now it's captured in a book. Theirs is the most helpful kind: the gritty, earthy wisdom learned in the hard school of real experience. Their transparency is refreshing and their good-humored, blunt counsel is gold. Dude, if you're going to read one book on marriage, read this one."

—Jon Bloom, cofounder and chair of Desiring God and author of *Not by Sight* and *Things Not Seen*

"Contrary to conventional wisdom, the secret to a great marriage isn't finding the right person. It's found in becoming the right person. Unfortunately, most of us guys enter marriage ill-equipped to be the kind of husband that great marriages are made of. *The Dude's Guide to Marriage* can change that. With refreshing candor and real-world wisdom, Darrin and Amie Patrick reveal the attitudes and skills that will make any husband, a better husband—and any marriage, a better marriage. I encourage you to read it. Carefully. You'll be glad you did. So will your wife."

—Larry Osborne, author and pastor of North Coast Church, Vista, California

THE DUDE'S GUIDE TO MARRIAGE

TEN SKILLS EVERY HUSBAND MUST DEVELOP TO LOVE HIS WIFE WELL

DARRIN AND AMIE PATRICK

NELSON BOOKS
An Imprint of Thomas Nelson

To our children—Glory, Grace, Drew, and Delainey:
We are so grateful for you and love being your parents.

Published in Nashville, Tennessee, by Nelson Books, an imprint of Thomas Nelson. Nelson Books and Thomas Nelson are registered trademarks of HarperCollins Christian Publishing, Inc.

Published in association with the literary agency of Wolgemuth & Associates, Inc.

Thomas Nelson, Inc., titles may be purchased in bulk for educational, business, fund-raising, or sales promotional use. For information, please e-mail SpecialMarkets@ThomasNelson.com.

Author photos courtesy of Lisa Hessel Photography.
Interior designed by James A. Phinney.

Library of Congress Cataloging-in-Publication Data

Patrick, Darrin, 1970-
The dude's guide to marriage : ten skills every man needs to love his wife well / Darrin and Amie Patrick.
pages cm
Includes bibliographical references.
ISBN 978-1-4002-0549-3
1. Marriage--Religious aspects--Christianity. 2. Husbands. 3. Wives. I. Title.
BV835.P378 2015
248.8'425--dc23

2015010664

Printed in the United States of America

15 16 17 18 19 RRD 6 5 4 3 2 1

CONTENTS

FOREWORD

I HAVE TO SAY, I LOVE THIS BOOK. THIS IS WHY I HAVE written this foreword. Yes, Darrin is a friend in ministry and I have recommended other things that he has written, but that is not why I decided to write this foreword. I was willing to take my time to do this because I so appreciate both the subject and the content of what you are beginning to read. Let me explain.

If you're committed to a ministry life, you will be exposed to things that make your heart grieve. This has happened to me over and over again in one particular area. I will be somewhere doing a marriage weekend and during one of the breaks a wife will come to me and say, "This is such helpful material, I wish I would've been able to get my husband to come with me." It crushes me every time I hear it. How can a marriage be healthy when the husband is so detached and inactive that he is unwilling to give up one weekend of his life to focus on it? Could it be that there really are men out there who would rather spend a weekend with their golf clubs, fly rods, shotguns, or tennis racquets than they would at a marriage conference with their wives? What must his wife think when he says no? What must she be thinking as she takes in the content of the weekend? And what must she be thinking as she hits the driveway loaded with new hope and enthusiasm for her marriage that she knows her husband doesn't share?

Here's why this is profoundly more important than missing one marriage conference. I am deeply persuaded that the number-one reason that marriages fail is not adultery or abuse, but *neglect*. Long before adultery takes place, shattering trust, and long before abuse makes the marriage a dangerous place, neglect has already sucked the life out of the marriage, and in so doing, set it up for difficulty and dysfunction of some kind. You see, you simply cannot have a sinner living with a sinner without focusing and working on your marriage all the time, any more than you can plant a garden and expect it to produce beautiful and healthy flowers without being committed to watering and weeding it.

Now, what I am going to write next is painful to write, but I must. It is my experience in almost forty years of pastoral ministry that dudes tend to be way more neglectful of their marriages than their wives are. There are hundreds of thousands of men every day who when they punch out from work essentially punch out from life. This means when they get home what they secretly want is to be left alone. They aren't arriving at home willingly and lovingly engaged in the daily maintenance work that it takes to make marriage all that God designed it to be.

So, that's why I love this book and think that it is so important for you and me to read, consider, and live. In this book, my friends Darrin and Amie not only have written a very provocative call to men to give themselves to their wives and their marriages, but they have also beautifully and practically detailed what that looks like.

Sin makes all of us selfish. It gives all of us antisocial instincts that are destructive to marriage. So God, in his amazing grace, not only forgives us but welcomes us to a brand-new way of living toward him and with one another. This new way of other-centered love is not natural for us. Selfishness is natural, entitlement is natural, demandingness is natural, disinterest in others is natural, irritation and impatience are natural, but it is simply not natural for us to willingly and patiently serve and love our wives as Jesus loves us. Men, for that to ever be natural, we need help.

Finally, I love this book because it preaches the gospel to every married dude who picks it up and reads it. I mean, come on, what man could honestly consider the lifestyle of self-sacrificing love that this book calls all of us to in our marriages and say, "Sure, I can do that, no problem"? When I read this book, I immediately thought, *This standard is too high; there's no way I am going to pull it off*, and then I remembered the right-here, right-now message of the grace of Jesus. This grace is the hope of every husband. "Why?" you ask. Let me explain.

This book is insightful and practical for every married man because it requires you to make one very humbling confession. What is that confession? It's that our biggest, deepest, most long-term problem in marriage, one that none of us can escape, is *us*! Now, you can run from a situation, you can run from a location, and you can run from a relationship, but you can't run from yourself. I've found that when I try to run from myself, I always show up with me at the end of the run!

So beneath the loads of wonderful, practical advice that you will find in this book is something deeper. It's a call to man up and admit your need for help and to seek and savor the help that is only ever found in the forgiving, enabling, and transforming grace of Jesus. That grace is yours for the taking, and with it a brand-new way of living. That new way is beautifully and clearly laid out for you, in the context of marriage, in the book you are about to read. Don't burn through it quickly. Take your time and let Darrin and Amie's words sink in, and then watch what God will do in you and in your marriage.

Paul David Tripp

President, Paul Tripp Ministries

"Connecting the transforming power of Jesus Christ to everyday life."

INTRODUCTION

IN A SOCIETY THAT HAS LOST ITS RITES AND RITUALS, getting married might be the clearest indicator that we are now indeed men. Think about it. We have somehow managed to convince a girl—and typically her father—that lifelong security and comfort can be found in our arms. This idea is exhilarating at first. But then it's frightening when you realize people actually expect you to deliver.

I know I was scared to death to get married. I had not seen a good marriage before I said "I do." I didn't know whether I was man enough to be a husband. Was I ready? Would we make it? We were happy at that time. Could we stay that way? These were just a few of my questions.

I am pretty sure that my parents were happy at some point in their marriage. My mom and dad met on a double date, only they weren't each other's date. During the course of the evening, my dad realized that he liked Karen more than his date for the night. So he arranged to take Karen home last. That night they had their first kiss.

Relatives have told me that my mom and dad enjoyed each other early in their marriage. They bowled together. They traveled together. They even did yard work together. But by the time I was in elementary school, it seemed that Mom and Dad had fallen into the "marriage-as-business" mode. I rarely saw them holding hands or expressing affection for each other. I can't remember them going on a date together. When I was twelve, they divorced.

I had been dating Amie (my wife) on and off again for several years when I finally had a conversation with my dad about his marriage. I asked him for tips on giving a woman what she wants. Dad was on his third wife at the time, and he said, "Darrin, all I know how to do is work! I'm not too good at all that romance stuff. I just try to provide and protect. That is all I know about marriage."

My dad was telling the truth. He was a classic provider. To this day, I have not met a man who worked harder than my dad. He worked all day doing excavation and then came home and worked on one of the many houses he built by hand. He understood work. He valued work.

All of us know something about how marriage works. We get some things right, as my dad did. But marriage is so scary because there is a lot we don't understand. The philosophy and principles found in this book are the things I wish I had understood before my wedding day. These are the words of wisdom I wish my dad had shared when I was twenty-two.

These are the words I often forget but am still trying to live out in my marriage.

If you are reading this right now, it is likely that your wife handed it to you. This is her way of helping you understand her better. Lest you think I've mastered this whole deal, know that you are going to hear from my wife throughout the book. Every once in a while, Amie will pop her head in the room and share her wisdom. You will know that something is her contribution because it is in italics. You're going to hear the glory and the garbage of our twenty-plus years of marriage.

We wrote this book for guys who want to grow. For guys who want to stop using their strengths to excuse their weaknesses. This is for guys who are not content with abstract ideas but are looking for concrete steps to become better men and, as a result, better husbands. This book has one-word chapter titles, focusing your attention on specifics so you can become the kind of man who loves a woman well.

This is for you if you want your marriage to thrive, not simply survive.

CHAPTER 1

LISTEN

Husbands, live with your wives in
an understanding way.
—1 Peter 3:7

WOMEN LIKE IT WHEN YOU LISTEN TO THEM. THEY ARE funny that way. My wife often asks if I hear what she says: "Are you really listening to me?" Many times I'm not. I mean, I am, but I'm not. I hear words coming from her cute, perky lips, but I often fail to listen to the heart behind those words.

The truth is I wish my wife wouldn't talk so much. She could say what she is trying to say with way fewer adjectives and superlatives. She knows how to get to the point. She is aware that I have a short attention span. She has studied my thoughts, actions, and words for twenty years. Yet she keeps talking.[1]

I'd rather be the one talking. I literally talk for a living. I traffic in words. There is nothing quite like standing up in front of fifty or five thousand people and uttering a profound, life-changing statement. To be able to hold the attention of people with my words is one of the greatest gifts I have been given. But there is a dark side to this gift. When I talk, I'm in control. I like being in control. I like giving directives. I like solving problems. Not every man has a job that requires public speaking, but every man uses words. We like to give our opinions, state our case, and instill our wisdom. We use words, and when we do, we feel like we are in control.

Proverbs 18:21 tells us, "Death and life are in the power of the tongue." Words are quite spiritual. We learn from the Bible that in the beginning God created the whole universe with a word. God reveals who he is through the created world generally, but through his words (the Bible) specifically. God has given us words to build a relationship with him. That's called prayer. Words aren't just organized noise coming out of our mouths. They are a spiritual force that has power.

Men and women use this controlling force in distinct ways. Men tend to view themselves as individuals in a hierarchical social order in which they are "either one-up or one-down."[2] Women usually view the world as a network of connections in which conversations are negotiations for closeness and consensus. Men talk with a focus on achieving social status and avoiding failure, while women focus on achieving personal connection and avoiding social isolation.

These different ways of conversing are known as *report-talk* (men) and *rapport-talk* (women). Report-talk is information oriented, focused on objectivity and practicality. Rapport-talk is relationship oriented, emotionally expressive, and engaging. When you come home from work, and your wife asks, "How was your day?" she is attempting to engage in rapport-talk. When you respond, "Fine," you assume she was looking for a report.

If you think having a wife who talks too much is the worst thing possible, wait until she stops.

WHY DO WIVES STOP TALKING?

Many husbands think their wives talking less is a good thing. Not so much. When your wife gives in to report-talk and stops trying to gain rapport, it doesn't mean you've won. It means she's no longer pursuing connection. If you think having a wife who talks too much is the worst thing possible, wait until she stops.

THEY DON'T FEEL SAFE

The other day I noticed Amie was especially silent. Later in the day that silence morphed into coldness. I could tell she had been hurt by something I had done. I racked my brain, trying to figure out how I had offended her. What had I done that morning? It turned out the offense had occurred earlier in the week. My wife was trying to express her feelings about an upcoming family event. I was preoccupied and said, "Amie, just figure it out. I'll do whatever you want." She interpreted this to mean, "Darrin doesn't care and is unwilling to engage with me about our family." Guilty as charged. She was right.

Because of her experiences with her husband and with counseling other women, Amie has some wisdom here.

A wife stops talking to her husband when she's given up hope that he will be a safe place for her to share her heart. She's probably resorted to having her need to be listened to met by someone else—girlfriends, Mom, coworkers, or even another man. The good news is that it's never too late to change course. A great place to start would be to tell your wife, "I know I'm a terrible listener and I've hurt you. I want to change. Will you help me?" She may not come around immediately, but genuine humility and vulnerability go a long way in healing broken places.

THEY ARE TIRED OF EXCUSES

Many wives have set the right environment, have tried to approach their husbands in the right spirit and at the right time, and have been given the Heisman (stiff-arm) multiple times. Husband, when conflict arises, you are far more likely to stonewall (shut down and become unresponsive). Faced with intense, troubling emotions, you will just sit there silently, trying not to react, just idling in neutral. You may not intend harm, but it is hard for your wife not to view it as disapproval and rejection.[3] Her knee-jerk response is to perceive your silence as hostility. A wife gets tired of pushing through her husband's walls.

THEY ARE TIRED OF BEING FIXED

Women want to be heard, not fixed. They are open to encouragement, challenge, and even rebuke, but usually only after they have been listened to. Research from Dr. John Gottman tells us, "Women are more sensitive to advice-giving than are men." A wife will usually react "very negatively" if you try to problem solve her troubles without trying to empathize.[4]

Amie has found it very helpful when I ask, "Do you want me to help solve the problem, or do you just want me to listen?" Ninety-eight percent of the time she just wants me to listen and understand her perspective. She is more open to proposed solutions if I have spent several minutes patiently listening to her.

THEIR HUSBANDS ARE DISTRACTED

Women do not want to engage in a conversation with a husband who is not focused. Your posture communicates attentiveness or inattentiveness. Eye contact communicates engagement. Most of the time when Amie asks me if I am listening to her, I'm not, though I often fudge and say I am. But sometimes I am listening. The problem is not that I'm listening and my wife doesn't recognize it. The problem is that I am not *communicating* that I am listening.

WHAT CAN HUSBANDS DO TO COMMUNICATE LISTENING?

I have learned to love listening to my wife. Over the years I have grown in how to show Amie that I am interested in understanding her heart through her words. I am learning to express affection for her and validate her emotions with my mouth closed and my ears open. The other day after Amie attended two of our kids' parent-teacher conferences, I asked her what the teachers said and what she felt about the interaction. Now, this was a huge step in that I actually engaged her heart (what she felt) and not just her head (what the teachers said). When she was talking, I made sure I was listening with my body. You can actually listen with your eyes, your face, and your words.

MAKE EYE CONTACT

This is the big *E* on the eye chart. Look at your wife. Focus on her eyes, which are windows into her soul. Her eyes will communicate even more than her words. Don't look through her, but look to her. Don't be afraid of her. Engage her face. My friend Dave Gibbons says, "If we paid as much attention to our wife as we do our phones, we would probably have a great marriage."

WATCH YOUR FACE AND BODY

As a public speaker, I am hyperaware of nonverbal communication. I try to zone in on a few individuals to see if my message is connecting. Are they engaged, or are they bored? Do I need to pause and be more descriptive? Do I need to omit a point that isn't relevant? How does the crowd give these cues? Nonverbals. When their arms are folded, faces frowned, eyes intent on their phones, they signal that they aren't engaged or don't know how to show that they are engaged. If I show my wife that I am interested in what she is saying with good nonverbals, I actually become more interested in what she is saying.[5] When your wife talks, nod, smile, lean forward, do whatever is appropriate to tell her you are interested in her perspective.

REPEAT, REPEAT, REPEAT

My wife and I went to college together. She was summa cum laude and the star of her class. Me? I squeezed four years into five. We had only a couple of classes together. But one of those was an intensive weekend class for intro psychology. I don't remember much about the class because I was staring at my wife during most lectures, but I do remember this helpful piece of advice from the prof: when someone says something to you, it is a good idea to repeat what the person said before you answer.

Act as if you are at a drive-through.[6] One person speaks, and the other repeats what he or she heard. Here is an example: "Honey, I'm tired of the way you come home from work and immediately sit in front of the TV. It makes me feel that the TV is more important to you than I am." Then the other person repeats, "Okay, so it bothers you when I come home and go right for the TV. It makes you feel unimportant."

See how that works? Now, a couple of other important points. Keep things in the first person (I) as much as you can, instead of the second person (you). Talk about how you feel and try not to be accusing. Talk in feelings and facts only. Don't give your opinions or assume you know how the other person feels. Just give your side.

TRUTHS THAT LEAD TO LISTENING

As a pastor, I hear all kinds of confessions, even though I'm not Catholic. There is something cathartic about telling another person your sins and struggles (James 5:16). When we confess sin, we agree with God that something is wrong. To confess is to acknowledge reality. If we are going to become good listeners, we have to tell ourselves the truth.

I DON'T KNOW WHAT SHE IS GOING TO *SAY*

I too often make this mistake. Even after twenty-five years of knowing Amie and twenty-plus years of being married to her, I am surprised by her words. Last summer we were sitting on the porch of a lake house we rented for a vacation, talking about how hard the last few months had been and complaining about how complicated our lives were. We were making plans for the fall, and I was saying that I was going to change my schedule and put my foot down and so forth. I thought Amie, the prototypical planner, was going to jump in and offer solutions for a better fall season. Instead, she said, "I think we shouldn't worry about tomorrow. We should just enjoy this day." Wow! She is refreshingly unpredictable. Part of the joy of marriage is that conversation breaks up the monotony and busyness of life.

I DON'T KNOW WHAT SHE *MEANS*

This one is a little tricky. It is difficult to hear what your wife is actually saying. At times, grasping the intended meaning of her words seems impossible. The drive-through method will help you, but you may still miss her heart.

For instance, one day Amie started talking about our kids' schedules. At the time, we had four kids in four schools! It was chaos to say the least. At our weekly planning meeting, she was describing all the activities our children would be participating in that week. I assumed that she wanted me to speak into the schedule and insert myself to help solve some of the logistical problems. She stopped me midsentence and said, "Darrin, I just want you to hear all that is going on with our kids. I want you to know what is going on with me and how I am managing everything. I don't need you to jump in and save the day. I just need you to listen to my heart." Words from your wife can be an invitation to know her deeply.

I DON'T HAVE TO SOLVE MY WIFE AS IF SHE IS A PROBLEM

Every guy acts like a math student with his wife. She isn't algebra, and thank God for that. She is, as one author noted, "not a problem to be solved but a vast wonder to be enjoyed."[7] When a wife knows that her husband is genuinely interested and engaged in the little details of her life, she will trust him more deeply with big decisions and significant life challenges.

Actively listening to your wife communicates that you want to understand her. You value her for herself, not just for what she does. Listening well affirms her character while shaping yours. Listening communicates a desire for partnership, where both husband and wife are known and are committed to each other's well-being above his or her own. A good husband, verbally and nonverbally, says to his wife, "You are worth hearing."

> Every guy acts like a math student with his wife. She isn't algebra, and thank God for that.

Five Good Questions

Before jumping into the next chapter, set aside some time to ask your wife the following questions. You'll find questions like these at the end of most chapters. This is your opportunity to initiate conversation with your wife and get another assessment of your strengths and weaknesses.

1. How would you rate my listening skills, 1 being awful, 10 being pure awesome? Why?
2. Who is the best listener you know? What makes him or her a good listener?

3. What practical things can I do to improve my listening skills?
4. Are there any bad listening habits that I need to drop?
5. What are the best times of day for us to have important conversations?

CHAPTER 2

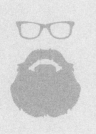

TALK

A soft answer turns away wrath,
but a harsh word stirs up anger.
—Proverbs 15:1

***FINE*. THAT IS MY GO-TO WORD. "HOW WAS WORK** today?" my wife asks. "Fine." "How was dinner?" "Fine." "How do I look in this dress?" "Fine." *Fine* is not such a fine word. My wife wants me to use verbs and adjectives when I talk to her. I bet your wife wants that too. My guess is our wives are worth talking to.

What is wrong with us, men? Why is it so easy to talk shop, sports, and lawn care with random strangers, and yet we can't speak meaningfully with our partners for life? If words are basically clothes for our thoughts, are we not thinking?

One of my roles as a pastor is to listen to people's problems and offer practical advice. A few years ago, Joe asked me to come to his office. He had something he wanted to discuss. I was escorted into his plush office as he was finishing up an overseas call.

As soon as I sat down, Joe launched into business matters. He talked about revenues and the growth of his business into emerging markets. He could see the top of the mountain and was actively planning to summit. I already knew he was a leader who was good at diagnosing problems and giving viable solutions. I learned that his specialty was seeing the subterranean issues in his industry and his staff. He was able to see motives, wounds, and other internal factors that most CEOs miss.

It took awhile before he disclosed the reason for my visit. He and his wife were struggling. She had confessed that she wasn't sure she was in love with him anymore.

I met with Joe several times during the next few months to explore the issues within his marriage, and he always talked about his business too. One day he was going on about the government regulations that would affect his business and the impact on the emotions of his staff. He had interviewed a couple of people who were familiar with governmental affairs. He described the thoughtful questions that he asked in the interview and how he engaged them personally about the potential ramifications on real people.

I took the opportunity to move from listening to talking

and interrupted him. "Joe, why don't you talk to your wife like that?" I asked.

"Like what?" he replied.

"Why don't you seek to understand your wife's heart by using words to draw her out?"

"What do you mean?"

"Why don't you seek to understand her motives and try to address her in her woundedness? Why don't you ask her about the impact that her past is having on your marriage?"

Joe looked at me, dumbfounded. He was great at engaging his business partners, but not great at connecting with his wife's heart. Joe is not alone.

WHY DON'T MEN TALK TO THEIR WIVES?

Why is talking to our wives one of the hardest things in the world for us to do? I have found there are conscious and unconscious reasons that keep us from communicating. Here are some specific reasons why we don't talk to our wives:

BROKEN ROUTINES

When I look back, I see that much of my lack of communication has to do with poor routines in talking with my wife. What worked once for Amie and me doesn't work any longer. It's hard for us to talk when I get home from work. We tend to default into my answering, "Fine," when she asks about my day, and then we immediately submit to the chaos of getting homework completed, dinner prepared, and bedtime stories read. We used to have great discussions after dinner. Then we began to connect before we went to bed. Now we are too tired. Currently we are trying early morning discussions, but that will probably change soon and we'll have to readjust again.

EMOTIONAL SHALLOWNESS

Men don't talk to their wives because they don't understand what is going on with themselves. A couple of years ago, I met with a communications consultant about how to improve my skill in public speaking. His central critique was that my nonverbal communication didn't match my words. He said, "Darrin, you just don't seem to be feeling the words you are speaking. We have to connect your emotions to your words." Most of the time, I felt nothing, even when using personal illustrations. The consultant suggested I do some work with a counselor. That may be something for you to think about (see appendix B). In counseling, I realized that because of past wounds and criticisms, I had disconnected my head and heart when I talked. I had learned to do a big part of my job without engaging my heart. This disconnect was sometimes apparent to those who heard me speak publicly. The disconnect was always apparent to Amie.

> Men don't talk to their wives because they don't understand what is going on with themselves.

When we don't know what we are feeling, or we are trying not to feel, our words will seem hollow and fail to connect.

VULNERABILITY

When Amie and I were first married, we talked about everything. I shared with her my hopes, dreams, and fears. It was natural and effortless. Over the years, we have lost ground in this area. Not because of her, but because of me. It has been a subtle shift, but I have found it increasingly difficult to open up to my wife.

If you are anything like me, your hopes, dreams, and fears are often wrapped up in your work. (I'll talk more about this later.) Back in 2002, we moved from Kansas City to start a church from scratch in St. Louis. In the first few years after planting the church, Amie was heavily involved. As our family and the church grew, I thought it was sensible to shield her from many of the concerns I was dealing with day in and day out. I reasoned that she had enough to deal with on the home front.

This seemed to be a legitimate way to protect Amie from my workplace chaos, but if I'm honest, I was also protecting myself from her. Sometimes I left her in the dark because I didn't want her to challenge and critique my plans. I kept my cards close to my chest (read: words in my mouth) so she could not use them against me.

The other day I was watching one of the dozens of reality shows about police investigation. The officer interrogating the suspect had a simple method: get the guy talking so that his words revealed the truth. The more the unsuspecting suspect talked, the more obvious it was that he had committed the crime.

I can almost guarantee your wife does not intend to lock you up. She's probably trying to get you to talk. My counselor does that. He asks a ton of questions to get me talking and expose my real issues. It is scary to be exposed, but it is also freeing. It takes courage to be vulnerable.

INTERPERSONAL AWKWARDNESS

Men don't know how to ask the right questions to engage the hearts of their wives. For years, I tended to ask questions that could be answered with one word. This tendency was illustrated in the *Seinfeld* sitcom of the 1990s. Jerry was trying to set George up with Nina, a good friend of his. George asked why Jerry and Nina never dated. Jerry answered that they got along so well together as friends and there were no "awkward pauses." George jubilantly replied, "I'm all awkward pauses!" A lot of husbands are like him. They were never taught and, therefore, failed to learn how to ask leading questions to bring out the best from their wives. Too many marital conversations are forced, uninteresting, and painfully awkward.

VERBAL EXHAUSTION

After engaging their coworkers all day long, many husbands just don't have any rich words in the tank for their sweet wives. The husband's word tank is almost on E, and the wife is experiencing fuel injection at 5:00 p.m.

This reality became clear to me when I was in graduate school and Amie was teaching music to middle schoolers. She spent most of the day teaching the same lesson several times to three hundred kids. She barely had any adult conversations. I spent all day in adult conversations as I went through my cohort-based program with twelve others. We spent nine hours a day interacting with one another and various professors. On top of that, I was teaching. I was all talked out by the time Amie came home hoping to have a conversation with someone who didn't pick his nose. It took us years to figure this one out.

MALE JARGON

Men don't know how to talk to their wives because they are only good at talking to men. I have two sisters, but growing up, I didn't have to deal with them much because they were ten and eleven years older than me. I mainly talked to male friends. Only around the seventh grade did it occur to me that I ought to learn how to talk to the ladies. I admit that my purpose in talking to girls wasn't exactly wholesome in those days. This, coupled with the fact that I didn't have any close friends who were girls through high school and college, made talking to my wife a big challenge.

> Men don't know how to talk to their wives because they are good at talking only to men.

WHAT DO WIVES WANT THEIR HUSBANDS TO TALK ABOUT?

I was talking to a friend the other day about how hard life is. Both of us have four young children, demanding jobs, and intelligent wives. We talk for a living. We were lamenting that we weren't connecting with our wives' hearts with our words. I began to think about what our wives really wanted from us. What do they want us to focus our words upon?

HEART, NOT ACTION

We men are action-oriented creatures, aren't we? We love to *do*. There is truth to the cleverly unclever statement, "We are human *be*-ings, not human *do*-ings." Husbands want to perform, accomplish, and "get 'er done." We don't want to talk about *why* we do these things or *how* we feel when we fail at these things. These are the exact things about which our ladies want us to spill the beans. They want us to talk about our failures and our motives. They want a peek into our hearts, not just our heads.

CONCERN, NOT SUCCESS

Our wives want to know what we are worried about, not just where we are succeeding. I can't tell you how frustrating it is when Amie doesn't do backflips as I report about all the wins I had from my job or my hobby. I can't tell you how surprised I am when she oozes empathy, attention, and support as I talk about my hopes, dreams, and fears. A wife wants to celebrate her husband's successes for sure, but in the context of understanding his concerns. When you are vulnerable with your words, your wife will in return be vulnerable with her heart.

HOME, NOT WORK

I like my work. I would do it for no salary. That is one benefit of working in your calling, not just pursuing a career or having a job. Because I like my job, I love to talk about it. I love to share the values and strategies that are making everything prosper. My wife loves when I talk family philosophy—defining and discussing the values that we hold dear. She loves to do strategery around how we are going to engage our kids' hearts and make memories for them. Her favorite word is *collaborate*. She delights when we talk about the locations of date nights, vacations, and overnight trips. Words clothe our passions. If we are passionate about our home life, the amount of our words and the energy behind them will reveal that.

HOW DO I TALK TO MY WIFE?

I don't know how many times I have incited an argument with Amie because of my words. More often it isn't the content (the *what* of my words), but rather the spirit (the *how* of my words) that gets me into trouble. So, *how* you say something is critical.

TALK, DON'T ACCUSE

Our wives want us to talk *to* them, not *at* them. They don't like lectures, and they hate accusations. Avoid saying words like *always* and *never.* Instead of giving answers and making proclamations, ask questions that draw your wife out. I speak and give answers to people for a living. You may do that too. Sometimes, what helps your business hurts your marriage.

BE CLEAR

If you want her to do something, don't hide it in metaphors and unclear words. This is a poor choice of words: "Honey, it would be great if the atmosphere at home had more positivity." This is a better choice: "Honey, I need you to be more encouraging by giving me specific, verbal affirmation regarding my success at work and my character at home."

Over time, I have realized that I crave feedback. I respect honesty. I tire of the insincere flattery and lack of truth telling so common in daily dialogue. I want my wife to be the one who gives it to me straight. We started using a feedback loop that has helped bring clarity to our conversations. Sometimes, we do this face-to-face. Other times, it's through e-mail and text.

We ask each other these three questions: (1) What should I keep doing? (2) What should I start doing? (3) What should I stop doing? They are simple but remarkable for achieving clarity in conversation. The other day Amie answered them for me: (1) Keep helping the kids with their homework. (2) Start helping more after dinner. (3) Stop checking e-mail from your phone.

USE PAUSES

Many guys dominate their wives with words, especially in an argument. They do this with logic, expertise, or tone.

A wise husband knows that winning an argument with his wife is not as important as winning her heart. I'm a quick verbal processor with a short attention span. Often many thoughts pulse through my brain at a given time. It's a struggle for me to stay focused on just one thing, particularly in a chaotic environment. Especially when I am stressed, I tend to get abrupt with my words and just want to get things done. It's important for me to pause often to give my wife space to process and respond. You'll need to do this as well, especially if your wife is an internal processor.

A wise husband knows that winning an argument with his wife is not as important as winning her heart.

KNOW WHAT MAKES HER FEEL DISMISSED

After about fifteen years of marriage, I finally asked Amie what made her feel belittled and dismissed. Then I asked her to ban certain activities of mine that harmed the community we were trying to build. Here's what she came up with:

- Walking out of the room without explanation when she's talking.
- Interrupting conversation by sending texts or e-mails or making notes "because I'll forget if I don't do it right now."
- Making her wait while I do something else when we've agreed to talk at a particular time.

- Trying to multitask during conversation (unless it's agreed upon).

THE POWER OF WORDS

Wives desire a heart-level connection with their husbands, and a significant portion of this happens through daily conversation. The heart and mouth are undoubtedly connected, and the way that we talk about ourselves, our circumstances, and others reveals a lot about us as people. The way that a husband chooses to use or not use the powerful gift of words in his marriage says a great deal about his character and love for his wife.

When Darrin is just reacting to situations, I can sense it in his words. When he's frustrated or anxious, I can hear it in his voice and see it on his face. When he's stressed and fatigued, he becomes terse and impatient. When he's hopeless, he gets sarcastic. And when he's afraid, he becomes frantic and demanding. If he is too overwhelmed to process his emotions, I can't trust him to be a safe place for sharing mine. But when Darrin puts forth the effort and discipline to reflect on his heart, he is able to ask inviting questions and speak words of encouragement and affirmation. His words have the power to draw us into greater intimacy.

My life is marked, as some of you have experienced, with words that I wish I would have heard but didn't hear. Hurtful words are remembered words. It's also the words that we wish we would have heard that we remember: "Son, you are doing a good job." "I am so proud of you." "You are the apple of my eye." Some of us have experienced deafening silence. We longed to hear certain words, but we never did.

I don't know about you, but I want my wife to hear the words she needs to hear. I don't want her to long for words and hear only frustration and silence. I want to speak life-giving words to her, words that only I can speak, words that say I trust you, I value you, and I want you.

Five Good Questions

1. Do I talk to you as much as you prefer?
2. When do we have our best conversations?
3. What are some topics that you would like us to spend more time talking about as a couple?
4. Do my words and tone generally feel kind to you?
5. How can we encourage more meaningful conversations in our family?

CHAPTER 3

FIGHT

Love without truth is sentimentality; it supports and affirms us but keeps us in denial about our flaws.

—Tim Keller

I GOT BEAT UP BY A GIRL IN THE FOURTH GRADE DURING recess. Gwen was offended because I was making fun of her height. "Hey, Gwen," I yelled, "how does it feel to be a giraffe?" Before I could say, "Uh-oh," Gwen was treating my face like a punching bag. In less than fifteen seconds and about thirty punches, I was lying on my back with a bloody nose and a bruised ego. The only thing more emasculating than living through that experience is telling you about it. Now, she was a tough girl, and I was a little guy. She was mad, and I was not. Still, that is an early age to have to turn in your man card. After that experience, I realized that if I was going to redeem myself on the playground of Washington Elementary School, I needed to learn how to fight.

I was always a good talker. I made people laugh. And I was a nice guy, if I do say so myself. The combination of all these things usually de-escalated potential physical altercations. But sometimes the only alternative was to face the conflict. I actually grew to enjoy conflict because it seemed easier to deal with the issue head-on rather than avoid it. I became a kid who took no guff from anyone. I didn't want to be known as the boy who got beaten up by a girl, so I became a fighter.

This strategy worked well until I met my wife in high school. We dated for several years before we married. We broke up, got back together, and then broke up again. We were too young. I had commitment issues. We had radically different personalities. We didn't have any mentors. Yada yada yada. The main problem in our relationship was that we didn't know how to deal with conflict. We weren't sure how to confront each other in our weaknesses. We had no skills to help us work through issues. We didn't know how to fight together. The truth is that you are going to fight. Are you going to fight well?

The truth is that you are going to fight. Are you going to fight well?

WHY DON'T COUPLES FIGHT WELL?

My wife and I had inadequate premarital counseling. Most people are jealous of us because they didn't have any. The guy who married us had great intentions and even probed into our motives for marriage. He asked us to consider the problems that might await us in the future and the concerns we had at that time. All good stuff, but we needed a deeper dive. We needed questions that looked into the future and also brought up our past.

Amie grew up in a house that was a sanctuary, meaning that her family saw the home as a place of refuge from the stress of daily life. Her parents were more private, and both of them worked. Consequently, Amie didn't have many friends spend the night with her, and very few guests came to the house. My home was an airport terminal. Familiar and unfamiliar people were always coming and going in my house. Unlike my dad, my mom was extremely extroverted. She stayed home and managed the house. Neither of our families was wrong or right.

Having these differences doesn't sound like a recipe for conflict, but in the early years of our marriage it was. I constantly invited people over to our tiny apartment, and Amie constantly wanted time with "just us." I felt confined, and she felt abandoned. After several years and three more apartments, we realized that our problems weren't products of our personalities or housing situation as much as products of our upbringings.[1] Couples don't know how to do conflict well for a multitude of reasons. But let's start with your upbringing.

YOUR FAMILY AFFECTS HOW YOU FIGHT

Some families ignore conflict and pretend it isn't there.

My friend Kyle grew up in a family like this. He and I shared two groups of friends. That's how we met. He was the link between the two tribes. Most of my friends in high school shared my affinity for fighting, except Kyle. He backed down from arguments and disappeared as soon as the first punch was thrown. For a year or so, I was at his house a few times a week. What I saw in Kyle, I also observed in his family. He confided that his parents were having money problems. I noticed the phone was always ringing when I was in his house. Those were creditors calling. I asked him if his parents ever discussed the problems with each other or with him and his sisters. He said, "No! We really don't talk about stuff like that." Maybe your family approached conflict like Kyle's.

Some families have fights only when the front line is at the front door.

That is, they engage conflict only when it's unavoidable. One of my college roommates and I both liked sports, and both of us were getting serious about our girlfriends. We had tons in common and lots to talk about. But we didn't talk about roomie issues. I was surprised that we hadn't had any fights as the semester neared its conclusion. Then one day I came back to the room after psychology class (the irony is thick), and he opened up a can on me. He was yelling while referencing a five-page treatise he had penned that outlined my roommate sins. He accosted me for a solid hour about leaving the faucet on, not replacing the cap on the toothpaste tube, and leaving expired milk in the refrigerator. He had been storing up all his bitterness, and he unloaded it on me when he couldn't take it anymore. When we both calmed down, I apologized for being a slob, and he confessed that he didn't know how to do conflict any other way. When I asked why, he said, "That's the way it was done in our family."

Some families make every little conflict an epic battle.

I got to know Marci in a semester-long class. The writing class included group projects about which we gave one another feedback. I noticed that Marci had difficulty with any feedback regarding her work. She took suggestions as attacks and turned critiques into opportunities to personally attack those who made amendments to her work. One day I was in the cafeteria line with her, and I asked her why she made every proverbial molehill into a mountain. She said, "I was taught not to show weakness and to fight anyone who pointed it out."

An awareness of how your family of origin dealt with conflict is invaluable if you are going to handle conflict well with your spouse. Whether you adopted your family's way or rebelled against it, knowledge is power in the fight to fight well.

YOUR PERSONALITY AFFECTS HOW YOU FIGHT

How you grew up matters, and so does how you are wired. Your personality influences you to moralize your preferred path in a conflict. You think the way you feel comfortable

In marriage, we are confronted with who we really are.

dealing with conflict is the *right* way.[2] Growing up was probably hard because it is likely that your whole family didn't approach conflict according to your liking.[3] As a single adult, I began to make relational choices to fit my conflict preferences. I wanted friends who didn't tiptoe around conflict and were willing to go at it on a regular basis. Many of us have surrounded ourselves with friends, roommates, and significant others who tolerate and even accommodate our strategies for fighting. This approach works pretty well until we get married.

Many husbands have witnessed their conflict philosophies crumble right before their eyes as they fight with their wives. What worked with our families or even our friends in conflict may not work with our wives. In marriage, we are confronted with who we really are. In marriage, our fail-safe strategies are exposed and found wanting. Many marriages struggle and die because of personality differences. Don't let that happen to you. God has wired you and given you your spouse as a lifelong partner, not a short-term combatant.

Personality Types

The key is to understand and recognize your personality and that of your spouse. It can be a rewarding and eye-opening experience to read each other's personality profiles together. Doing that has the potential to rearrange some of the mental furniture in how you relate to each other. You are not going to be able to change the way you've been wired, but you can learn to be more accommodating of your spouse.[4]

YOUR LIFE EXPERIENCES AFFECT HOW YOU FIGHT

I was barely twelve and not quite five feet tall. Most of my friends were bigger, stronger, and taller than I was and were starting to exert their physical dominance by picking on me and pushing me around between classes in the hall. One so-called friend felt the need to belittle me often, pun intended.

He mocked more than my height. My ears were too big. My nose was too small. And then he found the one spot where I was most vulnerable, and it had nothing to do with my physical appearance.

"Hey, Darrin," he asked, "why doesn't your dad come to your baseball games?"

Hearing that was worse than getting a punch in the gut. He knew my parents were in the midst of a divorce. I finally had enough. It was go time! I waited till the teachers were distracted and got face to chin with my bully on the playground. Fists would have flown if our friends had not intervened. My "friend" retaliated by gossiping about me to his parents' friends who happened to run a company that took junior high students to camp. He also ran me down to the guys who operated the concession stand at the ballpark. As a result, I wasn't picked to go on a couple of cool trips and didn't have a summer job for two years. That happened because he told them I was a bad kid.

Around that time I began to question my approach to conflict. Even as a prepubescent boy, I began to wonder if conflict was really worth it, especially as I was watching my parents' marriage disintegrate. I started believing this equation: conflict = loss. We all have an equation about conflict, a philosophy that fuels our approach to it.

Three Patterns of Communication Breakdown[5]

Dr. Sue Johnson, a clinical psychologist, suggests that couples replay three basic patterns of communication time and time again when conflict arises and they cannot safely connect with each other.

1. Find the Bad Guy

   This occurs when spouses accuse or blame the other for the current conflict. This "dead-end pattern" keeps spouses at arm's length, blocking reengagement.

2. The Protest Polka

   This is the most common pattern, which marriage researchers have labeled as "Demand-Withdraw" or "Criticize-Defend." When spouses fear that they've lost connection, they will go into fight-or-flight mode. One partner will do anything to provoke a response. When the other partner perceives this as failure, he or she will begin to freeze up.

3. Freeze and Flee (Withdraw-Withdraw)

   This is the eventual response to the "Protest Polka," when both spouses lose hope in the relationship. Giving up, they begin to put their emotions and needs in the deep freeze, leaving only numbness and distance.

WHEN YOU MARRY YOURSELF . . . OR THE OPPOSITE

A major concern Amie and I had as we were approaching marriage centered on our dramatic personality differences. We are still dealing with those differences because temperament doesn't really change.[6] We did, however, see eye to eye on numerous subjects. We had very similar views of spirituality, recreation, and lifestyle. We've had little conflict in these areas. And when there has been conflict, we've been able to help each other navigate the waters of marriage.

You will also fight about the areas where one partner is strong and the other is weak. I grew up in a broken home. My mom did the best she could to raise me, but having only one involved parent hurts a kid. Mainly because of my bitterness and rebellion, I didn't learn how to be empathetic to others who are struggling. I was always in "fix it" mode, not "feel it" mode. If someone was hurting, I listened just long enough to give instructions on how to get better. Amie grew up with two parents who listened, loved, and supported her. They weren't perfect, but they modeled how to listen and connect emotionally with others. She has great strength to connect with the heart of a person.

Two of my friends pretty much married themselves. Both hate structure, preferring to live in the moment, and both had jobs that accommodated their preferences. Being friends with them was a ton of fun because they were so flexible. They were up for anything. This laissez-faire philosophy worked until they had a child. Kids need structure and demand discipline. Our friends nearly divorced trying to reorganize their lives. They were drawing water from a well that was dry because both were weak in the same area. Consequently, they fought all the time because neither partner could really help the other.

Whether you married yourself or your opposite, there are opportunities and challenges to fight for a good marriage in the realm of disagreement and conflict.

FIGHTING THE GOOD FIGHT

Darrin and I have struggled mightily learning how to fight well. He's much more comfortable with conflict than I am. In the fight-or-flight model, he's a fighter, and I'm a flier. He's willing to jump right into the pool fully clothed, while I'm looking for a way not to get my hair wet. Even when a situation arises that makes a hard conversation inevitable, I resist being the one to start talking about the issue. Overall in my life, I've seen conflict be more ugly and destructive than positive and redemptive, so my first instinct is to avoid it whenever possible.

Darrin and I operate at different paces when it comes to processing information and then communicating about it. Darrin is quick verbally. He can put words to his thoughts and articulate them much faster than I can. If I have time and space to think first, communicating well is easy, but when I am forced to figure something out in a hurry, I become increasingly panicked and stuck. The more that Darrin keeps talking and explaining himself, the more I want to run from the room. He's also a verbal processor. He figures out what he actually thinks by testing several versions of it out loud. I've found it nearly impossible to wade through all of what he's saying and decide which version most reflects his intentions. It's been very challenging to ask him to be accountable about what he says, while also giving him freedom not to explain himself perfectly on the first try. And I've found it impossible to formulate my response while simultaneously trying to understand his!

There have been seasons in our marriage when we've wondered if we'll ever be able to overcome our differences and learn to fight well. Here are a few things we've learned over time:

STOP VIEWING EACH OTHER AS ENEMIES

It's helped us a lot to remind each other that we're on the same team, even in the middle of an argument when it feels as if we're standing on opposite sides of the field. Going back to the big values that we have in common and working forward from there sometimes feels as if we are working backward, but it's much better than getting stuck in the details on which we may never completely agree.

Early in our marriage we had a fight that started out about clutter but was really about deeper and bigger things. We spent most of a day letting tension build between us while we were busy with other things, and then we both exploded in anger. Because Darrin is so good with his words, it's rare for me to find any holes in his very persuasive arguments right away. But this time, I quickly realized that the clutter on the dresser that he was complaining about consisted entirely of items that belonged to him. Finally, I could win! I dramatically picked up each item, threw it on the floor, and loudly stated the obvious: "And who does this one belong to? Not me!" I didn't even try to hide my pleasure in proving him wrong.

At that point, Darrin calmly suggested that perhaps clutter was not the real issue. It was that neither of us felt valued or appreciated by the other. I was more than a little irritated that he didn't recognize my victory, and I'm pretty sure that Darrin's motives behind turning the tables in that moment weren't completely pure. Nevertheless, I had to admit that he was right. He was right about the deeper truth, and he was right to bring us back to it.

We've had to let go of some bad habits and divisive strategies related to conflict. Darrin tends to use his quickness to back me into a corner, and I've used my thoughtful slowness to build a huge case against him and then attack him out of the blue. Both strategies are selfish and unhelpful.

Darrin is learning to give me space in the form of silence and compassionate listening. When I know that he's really trying to listen, giving me space to process, and exercising self-control, I'm much more willing to be vulnerable. And my genuine brokenheartedness has spoken louder to Darrin than the most careful and organized argument that I could ever prepare. A simple and humble "You really hurt my feelings" or "I miss you" isn't flashy or dramatic but speaks volumes. Additionally, his willingness to examine his issues with anger and impatience and let go of his tendency to use his persuasive verbal skills for his benefit has spoken more powerfully to me than anything he could ever say to win an argument.

AVOID ARGUING WHEN YOU'RE DEPLETED

It's almost always dangerous to enter into conflict when you're depleted on a physical, mental, emotional, or spiritual level. Sometimes it's unavoidable, but when at all possible, it's better to take a break, get a little rest, or do something replenishing instead of making immediate resolution the goal. We've found the HALT acronym to be extremely helpful.[7] *If you're hungry, angry, lonely, or tired, it's better not to dive into a contentious discussion. When any of those factors are present, we tend to say things we don't really mean and lose sight of the bigger goal, which is working as a team toward common goals and the good of each other.*

We've had to humbly admit that many skills related to healthy conflict resolution didn't come naturally to us and that we needed help from wise and trustworthy people in order to learn and grow. We've had to step out of our comfort zones and dive into the messiness of working things out slowly and painfully over time. We've had to apologize, start over, take a break, apologize again, and keep trying.

LET GO OF THE NEED FOR AN IMMEDIATE SOLUTION

The best thing that Darrin has done for me as a husband is to own the idea that there's a bigger purpose to conflict than just solving the problem at hand or getting his way. Conflict exposes our hearts and helps us know each other as few other things can. As Darrin has understood and owned the vision of conflict as a means to help us develop a more intimate marriage and a more surrendered personal relationship to God, my love for and trust in him have grown exponentially. It's easier for me to bring a potentially difficult topic to Darrin when I see him letting go of his desire to solve every problem right now and instead embrace the process of allowing conflict to expose difficulties that we can work through together.

It's almost always dangerous to enter into conflict when you're depleted on a physical, mental, emotional, or spiritual level.

RULES FOR FIGHTING FAIR

Fighting fair involves having agreed-upon rules to which each person submits. These are boundaries that enable spouses to feel safe enough to enter into conflict, even when emotions run high.

ARTICULATE THE OTHER'S POINT

Back in chapter 1, "Listen," I talked about learning only one thing from a particular class (because I spent most of the time staring at my future wife): the need to repeat the concern of your spouse before responding. Remember Gary Smalley's drive-through communication method? Well, the technique (also called mirroring[8]) is helpful when applied to conflict. Simply put, don't argue with your wife until you can clearly demonstrate empathy toward her point of view.

STATE YOUR SIDE HUMBLY

Being confident when I argue my side is easy for me because I speak in front of crowds for a living. Over the years I have perfected my ability to hold the attention of hundreds and sometimes thousands of people. I know how to transition seamlessly from one illustration to another, when to pause after making a point, and how to raise my voice at precisely the right moment for maximum impact.

But crowds don't talk back. My wife does. Crowds enjoy it when I raise my voice. My wife doesn't. Crowds love dramatic pauses. My wife? Not so much. She sees through me. She also knows all my tricks, and when I try to persuade her like a congregant, she feels as if I am preaching at her instead of connecting with her. When I temper my confidence with humility, my wife responds.

LET THE GOAL BE UNITY, NOT WINNING

One reason I quit playing basketball is that I would frequently get in a fight or get hurt. Both options are bad, especially the first one, as a pastor. My problem is that I want to win in almost everything. Yet even in professional sports, how teammates play together is the indicator of how many wins they get. Chemistry is usually the intangible behind championships. When you are in a conflict with your wife, remember that unity is better than one victory. Winning one argument is not winning if you lose any part of your wife's heart.

Winning one argument is not winning if you lose any part of your wife's heart.

REALIZE THE FIGHT IS ABOUT MORE

Even a small conflict will teach a couple about themselves. Fights reveal what offends us. Fights reveal what we are passionate about. Fights disclose hidden motives by which we tend to operate. There is a saying, "If you really want to get to know people, argue with them." This is true. Fights show us who we really are and help us to be better than we are.

Fighting with Amie has taught me more about her than just about anything. She hates conflict, especially with me. But her best character qualities come out when we fight. Amie is extremely articulate, and when she has time to respond, her clear communication highlights her intelligence. Also, the way she chooses her words reveals her thoughtfulness and compassion. Although Amie is pretty even-keeled, she can get loud. I love this because I sense her passion for life.

Five Good Questions

1. What was our worst fight?
2. Where do I not fight fair?
3. Where am I avoiding conflict?
4. What do you wish I would stop doing when we fight?
5. What do you wish I would start doing when we fight?

CHAPTER 4

GROW

Get busy living or get busy dying.

—"Red" Redding, *The Shawshank Redemption*

PART OF BEING ALIVE IS GROWING. AT SOME POINT, USUally in our early twenties, we stop getting taller. But we never stop growing physically. I'm not just talking about our waistlines! Our brains can continue to grow into old age.[1] Even if we start losing the hair on our heads, we start growing hair in our ears! Growth in one form or another will happen.

Growth may be best observed in children. I love the process of growth in mine, but I would love it to speed up at times. That is when Amie assures me, "They'll get there." I want instant growth. I am a microwave guy, not a Crock-Pot guy. Most growth comes intentionally, not naturally. And it is easy to get stuck. Just ask my wife.

Darrin is primarily a type A go-getter who doesn't hesitate much in tackling problems and busting through roadblocks. His emotional health, however, is an area where I've seen him be less than his normal aggressive self. The early years of planting and pastoring our church were incredibly demanding. Darrin had eighty-hour workweeks, and we weathered a lot of difficult circumstances in a relatively short time. People left, including ones we thought would always be around, there was always a new problem related to facilities or money, and our young family was growing rapidly, as was our young church. The demands on our time and energy felt relentless.

When several years of significant stress started to take a toll on Darrin's physical and emotional well-being, he quickly started problem solving on the physical side, but I didn't see much happening on the emotional front. He was angry, somewhat hopeless, and difficult to live with. I was frustrated by the tone he was setting in our home for our family, as well as his lack of emotional engagement with me. I soon realized that he knew there was a problem, but he didn't know what to do about it. So he didn't do anything. Darrin could not rely on his natural strengths and abilities in this area, so he grew stagnant. Doing nothing prolonged the damage of Darrin's unhealthy emotional life on our family.

My wife knew I wasn't growing. My friends knew I wasn't growing. And eventually I recognized the problem. I didn't know what to do in part because of self-deceit and in part because I didn't have a holistic definition of growth.

GROW INTELLECTUALLY—DEVELOP YOUR MIND

I wouldn't say that I was discouraged to write a book for men about marriage, but I wasn't exactly encouraged. I spoke with several people in the publishing world, and almost to a person they asked why I would write a book to men when men don't read books.[2] I used to be one of those men. Growing up, I was the quintessential dumb jock. I made it through high school without having to read an entire book. Only in college did I start cracking the books. I bet you read a book or twenty in college. But I would also bet that you haven't read much since then.

WHY MEN DON'T READ

- "I don't have time"—You make time for what is important. Men read and study for hobbies and work and information on how to fix stuff around the house.
- "I don't know where to start"—As you read this book, identify which chapters reveal your weaknesses. Start reading there.
- "I don't want to"—You do plenty of things that you don't want to do, and you learn to love many of them. Some of them, you don't. Discipline is important no matter what.

President Harry S. Truman once said, "Not all readers become leaders. But all leaders must be readers."[3] To grow intellectually, you are going to have to develop your mind by reading. I am not encouraging you (at least at first) to read about things in which you have little to no interest. My guess is that you could learn more about many things of interest to you.

> To grow intellectually, you are going to have to develop your mind by reading.

Someone asked me a few years ago about my hobbies. I replied, "Hobbies? I don't even have *a* hobby." Back then, I felt sorry for people who had to have a hobby. I thought if my work fulfilled me, and I was investing adequately in my family, I wouldn't need a hobby. Now I know how stupid I was. The desire to pursue a hobby sprung from a desire to quell the boredom and obsession with my job. I needed a new challenge. So I started rock climbing. There is nothing like realizing that the weight of your entire body is literally at your fingertips.

Rock climbing demands complete focus, which is just what I needed to forget about the stress of my job. My mentor owned a gym and led outdoor tours. He taught me technique and suggested I buy special pointed-toed shoes that helped me climb like a goat. On my own, I purchased books and magazines and watched countless videos to stoke the fire of my new hobby.

It is likely that you can find books, periodicals, and articles related to your work industry. Maybe you are bored with your industry, and you should research another one that might appeal to you. Maybe something in world history grabs you. Perhaps economic challenges spark your curiosity. A friend got interested in microeconomics and has become an expert in the field. He spent time in China while he was working on his MBA and was fascinated by the Chinese economic system. He used this newfound expertise to think through a business venture that he now leads with a dozen employees.

Amie and I have four kids; three are girls. Someone once said, "You cannot parent your children. You can only parent each child." I have found this to be true and troubling. If I am going to be the best parent I can be, I have to discern what each child needs in a given situation, adapt my parenting style to meet those needs, and do all this while controlling my emotions. Good luck with that, pal. This is why I am always reading (with my wife's strong encouragement and resourcing) about parenting. If you are married or want to be, you should read books on marriage. (Oh, wait, you are.)

GROW SOCIALLY—DEVELOP YOUR NETWORK

It was one of the few smart things I did in college: develop friends who weren't like me. Until then, almost all my friends shared my interests. Many of my buddies were jocks. I had fallen into the trap of the affinity network.[4] Most groups are rooted in affinity when they first begin, but they can easily become cliques. When that happens, affinity becomes less about having common ground and more about surrounding yourself with people who are like you to remind you how great you are.[5]

My first day in the dorm at college, I made a choice to seek community, not affinity. Community is diverse, disturbing, and challenging, unlike affinity, which is bland, reinforcing, and safe. I met a man who was, in his own words, a book nerd and didn't like sports. I befriended another man who was ten years older than me and had been a farmer. He taught me how to be patient with circumstances and people. I hung out with another person who was an extreme introvert. He avoided crowds and almost had a nervous breakdown when he had to speak in front of the class. He taught me how to be quiet and to enjoy being alone. I never would have chosen these guys as friends based on common interests because we didn't have that many. There is a saying, "Old friends are like old mirrors and new friends are like new mirrors." Sometimes new friends help us see things about ourselves that old friends don't.

Recently, I realized that I hadn't made a new friend in a couple of years. Earlier I mentioned the rock-climbing guru. He would prefer to live in the woods, which he once did for several months straight. His life is very simple. He runs his business (the gym) and pursues his passion (climbing). He refuses to allow the complexities of life to distract him from simplicity. I am learning from him about how to stay focused and enjoy my life. He says he learns from me about management and start-up issues with his business.

I have a new friend who is one of the top cartoonists in

the world. He is a *New York Times* bestselling author, and two of his books are being turned into movies. He also happens to be the dad of my daughter's best friend. We cowork a couple of times each month and share ideas. I even take him rock climbing and help him with his fear of heights. He helps me think outside the box with my writing. We help each other with strategies to keep the boys away from our daughters until they are thirty.

One of my neighbors sells insurance and is trying his best to raise his family. We have barbecues together and talk almost daily when it's warm outside. His kids are a little older than mine, so I ask him questions about surviving the teen years and how to stay connected to your wife after a few decades of marriage. He talks to me about spiritual things. We both complain about our local sports teams' lack of signing potential free agents.

One of the best things a man can do is get new mirrors. You might have to break up some of your cliques to do so, but you might enhance your community when you do. It is easy to say, "Get new friends!" But what kinds of guys should you seek?

FUN BROTHERS

New friends can bring fun back into your life. I used to be a pretty fun guy, but I got overly serious as my responsibilities multiplied. I compounded the problem by attracting a bunch of people around me who were also taking life too seriously. I am trying to surround myself with people who take their work and families seriously but refuse to take themselves so seriously. Fun brothers may be coworkers, golf buddies, or neighbors. With such men, we might participate in sports, share a hobby, or coach Little League. When we leave them, we feel more alive because we recapture what it was like to be little boys without a care in the world.

BUSINESS BROTHERS

The truth is that we spend more time with our coworkers than we do with our families, so it is helpful to actually have relationships with them. Finding a few dudes at work to confide in, share ideas with, and go to lunch with is a wise move. Doing this may not be possible for you because of the nature of your work. Maybe you are the sole employee of a start-up or you are in a family business and the relationships are already conflicted without trying to bring friendship into it. If you are in one of those situations, you need to go outside your business to find some brothers. Surely, others are doing something similar to what you are doing or are in a role that is similar to yours.

I am trying to surround myself with people who take their work and families seriously but refuse to take themselves so seriously.

SOUL BROTHERS

This is a fancy way of saying that you need real friends. It is easy to find guys who will tell us the truth but aren't willing to support us as we live the truth. It is also easy to find guys who will support us emotionally but aren't willing to honestly confront us about weakness. A soul brother does both truth (telling us the reality about ourselves and our situation) and love (being willing to walk with us into reality). The Bible encourages us to embrace the truth: "Better is open rebuke than hidden love. / Faithful are the wounds of a friend; profuse are the kisses of an enemy" (Prov. 27:5–6).

Recently someone I work with wounded me. He talked about how he thought I was working outside my gifting and suggested that I stop trying to lead a certain part of our organization and focus on the areas I was best suited to lead. This challenge (from a subordinate!) required me to make major adjustments. My coworker was firm and gentle and challenged me to stop hurting our mission and listen to his suggestion. That, my friends, is a friend.

As I discussed in *The Dude's Guide to Manhood*, friends know your hopes, dreams, and fears.[6] They don't stay on the surface; they go deep. And they are committed to helping you conquer your fears, live out your dreams, and grow in your character. True friends know you and want to be known by you. They celebrate you and are willing to be celebrated by you. They challenge you and seek to be challenged by you. And they serve you and are willing to be served by you.

I don't want to lose my current friends, but I do need new mirrors.

GROW EMOTIONALLY—DEVELOP YOUR HEART

You imitate the manhood lived out before you. I had my dad, three uncles, and two grandfathers. All were blue-collar, put-on-your-own-roof, change-your-own-oil, and get-it-done dudes. I can count on two fingers how many times I saw them cry. The not-so-subtle message: crying is for women and children.

On the other hand, these men were very tuned in to anger. In a thousand ways, most of them while working on cars or houses, my male models taught me to express anger. I remember hammers and fists being thrown, and language being used that would make Hollywood blush. I was taught to express my anger, apologize if necessary, and then move on. Not exactly the picture of emotional health, but at least I knew what anger was. It wasn't modeled, nor was it taught, that there were other emotions that a man should seek to engage and negotiate.

I have a friend who came from a home that provided him with a few more tools. I met him in college and was amazed at the breadth of his emotional responses to various situations. I was great at anger and terrible at empathy. Rob could be appropriately angry but could turn on a dime and experience extraordinary patience. I learned why. He grew up with a dad who was an accomplished artist and a mother who was an elementary schoolteacher. He also had two older sisters. His family had long discussions during dinner, and each person shared what happened during the day.

The person who was sharing held a wooden spoon, which meant he or she had the floor. The other family members asked questions of the one holding the sharing spoon. The questions were more inviting than penetrating. The most common question was: How did that make you feel? Everyone was expected to identify, process, and respond to his or her emotions from the day. These discussions trained Rob to engage and talk not just about events from his day but also about his internal and external responses to his life. Doing this enabled Rob to share his fears, hopes, and dreams with those close to him.

My guess is that your experience is closer to mine than to Rob's. Most men weren't taught how to identify and respond appropriately to the emotions that are unearthed through challenges. More than likely, you don't know how to deal with anger, fear, worry, and grief, which is evidenced in the way you struggle to be warm and affectionate with some people and to be decisive and firm with others. You may have the wooden spoon in your hand, but you don't quite know what to say.

Many men don't know what to do when they are really happy any more than they know what to do when they are really sad. Some of us are terrible at taking compliments. Others are destroyed by critiques. In each case the heart has decreased in size as it has disengaged emotionally. Men are like old cars with engine troubles when it comes to emotions. Oil, antifreeze, and transmission fluid leak out slowly—or worse, all at once! Emotions are the same way. If we don't pay them attention, if we don't acknowledge them and talk

Men are like old cars with engine troubles when it comes to emotions. Oil, antifreeze, and transmission fluid leak out slowly—or worse, all at once!

about them, they'll leak out in our snarky comments or our passive-aggressive swipes at our friends, spouses, or kids. Or we'll just blow up, putting those around us in danger and creating an environment of fear and uncertainty. That is why we have to grow our hearts.

If you want to move toward health, you can start working on two basics:

STOP STUFFING DOWN YOUR EMOTIONS

You can't keep grabbing for the wet blanket every time intense emotions flare up. It's not just harmful for you individually; it's harmful for your marriage. The effort you exert to avoid your emotions is exhausting. It also distracts you from picking up on and responding to the emotional cues from your spouse. Stanford psychologist James Gross has shown that the tension created by suppressing emotion is contagious. Your spouse will catch your strain and become stressed as well.[7]

NAME YOUR EMOTIONS

This isn't about being clever. We're not talking about naming your sports car. Naming is recognizing. Through brain imaging technology (MRIs), UCLA psychologist Matthew Lieberman has shown that the simple act of naming calms the emotional center of the brain.[8] Dr. Sue Johnson said, "What we name we can tame; when we give meaning to something, we can tolerate it and even change its impact."[9]

Jeff Schulte of the Sage Hill Institute lists eight core emotions. When we ignore them, they become destructive (left column). When we name and use them properly, they become virtues (right column).

Depression	ANGER	Passion
Rage Control Anxiety	FEAR	Faith
Resentment	HURT	Healing Courage
Self-Pity	SAD	Acceptance (ok w/ what is not ok)
Apathy	LONELY	Intimacy
Toxic shame	GUILT	Forgiveness Freedom
Toxic shame	SHAME	Humility
Sensuous/sensual experience w/o heart	GLAD	Joy (w/sadness)

Feelings Chart © Dr. Chip Dodd *The Voice of the Heart: A Call to Full Living*

GROW SPIRITUALLY—DEVELOP YOUR SOUL

Spirituality is frustrating. Before and after becoming a follower of Jesus, I felt confined by spiritual practices. I was told I had to pray, read the Bible, and tell others about my faith if I wanted to mature. I was good at reading and talking to people but not so much at talking to God.

For years I felt like a junior-varsity Christian because I wasn't good at living out certain aspects of my faith. Fast-forward a few years. I am sitting in a leadership seminar, and I hear news that helped set me free. The speaker mentioned a book that was helping him grow in his spirituality. It was *Sacred Pathways* by Gary Thomas.[10]

Over several decades Thomas asked people a simple question: When do you feel closest to God? He received similar answers, which he labeled as pathways—the various ways that people connect with God. Thomas is a Christian writer, so he is not talking about different pathways to God in general but specific ways to connect with God through the person of Jesus.[11]

Some people are chronically bored because they are lazy. But many want to grow spiritually; they just don't have the tools. God has wired each person in a unique way. When we're unable to engage God through our unique wiring, spiritual maturity becomes elusive. *Sacred Pathways* helped me. I commend it to you. For our purposes, here is my adjusted summary of the pathways:

1. naturalist: Your spirituality is most real when in nature.
2. relational: God is most real when you are with people.
3. service-oriented: You feel most alive when you serve people in God's name.

4. intellectual: You sense God's presence when reading or discussing issues.
5. music-oriented: You feel closest to God when singing or listening to music.
6. activist: You sense God's pleasure when leading others to a good cause.
7. contemplative: God is near when you are alone and away from distractions.

I'm guessing that one or two from this list appeal greatly to you. Throw yourself into these main pathways. But let your favorite pathways lead you to the more difficult ones. In the ancient wisdom of the Bible, all these pathways and more are commanded to help us connect with the God who loves us.

What does a wife want? A growing husband. Growing husbands help their wives grow because they invite them to join them on their paths. Wives tend to respect husbands who do the hard work of moving courageously into areas where they're not naturally strong and doing the hard and humble work of learning and growing. Most look for persistence, not perfection. Wives trust their husbands more readily in difficulties and crises when they see their men regularly looking outside themselves for support.

Five Good Questions

1. In which area do you see me pursuing growth the most (intellectual, emotional, spiritual)?

2. How do I respond to your encouragement toward growth?
3. Which of my friends are the most encouraging and challenging?
4. Can you think of an area where we could grow together as a couple?
5. Are there areas in my life where you feel that I've become stagnant?

CHAPTER 5

PROVIDE

If anything can go wrong, it will.

—Murphy's Law

JASON AND REBECCA CAME FROM LOVING, SUPPORTIVE families. Both families were upper middle class, and the parents enjoyed success in their respective careers. Jason and Rebecca were thirty-one and twenty-nine, respectively. Rebecca was a midlevel executive at a Fortune 1000 company. She was rising very quickly in her company, but she wanted to have children. Jason was a young businessman working for his uncle's insurance company. When Jason's uncle tapped him to take over the business, he was in a great position to advance his career and provide for his family.

This couple arrived in my office for premarital counseling. During one session Rebecca lost it. She exclaimed, "I don't think I will ever be able to quit work, have kids, and enjoy my life."

"Why?" I asked.

"Jason just doesn't work hard. I don't think his uncle thinks so either. He has this good job in this great company, and he doesn't want it. He's not motivated. He won't work as hard as he could. He is just coasting."

Jason did not disagree with his soon-to-be bride. I asked what was getting his time and devotion. Jason talked about his passion for his college buddies who gathered once a year in some exotic place to party and reconnect. He described how much he enjoyed his weekly excursion to his private golf club. Jason's face lit up when he talked about his CrossFit regimen that took several hours of his week.

WHY MEN STRUGGLE WITH WORK

Jason and Rebecca represent one of the more unsettling trends I've noticed in my last ten years of counseling. The future wife is concerned about the lack of or misplaced ambition of her future husband. What was virtually nonexistent in my first decade of counseling has become the norm. Many men, like Jason, don't give themselves fully to their work. Guys are struggling to give the maximum effort in their jobs and careers and are subsequently undercutting their responsibility to provide. What's going on?

MEN HAVE NOT BEEN TAUGHT TO WORK

One consequence of our fatherless society is that most men haven't been adequately mentored by their dads, and they have prolonged their adolescence. For some guys, thirty has become the new twenty. According to sociologist Michael Kimmel, demographers used to cite "five life-stage events to mark the transition to adulthood: leaving home, completing one's education, starting work, getting married, and becoming a parent."[1] When these markers were first being used in the 1950s, most guys passed through them around the same time. But the passage between adolescence and adulthood has morphed from a transitional moment to a separate life stage. Several factors are involved, but I'm convinced guys who are not mentored well perceive adulthood only as hardship and drudgery.

My dad was probably the hardest-working man I have ever been around. Because my dad worked all day and then came home and worked some more, I had to work if I wanted to spend any time with him. He didn't quite know what to do with me. He was a worker, not a teacher. I just hung out at the job site and tried to figure out what he wanted me to do. Consequently, I learned the value of hard work without learning how to work hard. It took me many years to learn that I had to work hard and not just rely on fortunate circumstances or natural talent.[2]

Other men had dads who were absent from the home. They had no male role models to demonstrate hard work, much less instruct them in it. The number of men who have no dad around has increased exponentially.[3] A friend of mine grew up in the inner city of Saint Louis, which is regularly cited as one of the most dangerous cities in the United States.[4] His dad left shortly after he was born. When he was five, his dad was killed in a drug deal. He saw him only twice. I had to hold back tears as my friend described what it was like to grow up in a tough neighborhood. He had no dad to model for him or teach him anything about providing for his family. Guys in the neighborhood who were always chasing shortcuts to easy money rather than disciplining themselves to become lifelong providers were the ones who fathered him.

Some men had good dads, but their dads hated their jobs. Another friend had a dad like that. His dad always coached his sports teams. He always included him in home projects, patiently teaching his son how to keep a house together. One summer they even rebuilt an engine on an old Ford truck that both of them picked out in a junkyard. My friend's dad loved being with him, but his dad had nothing good to say about his job. Most of the time when he and my friend were riding together in the car or working around the house, his dad complained about his job. The only thing he criticized more than his working conditions was his supervisor. The not-so-subtle message that was sent to his son was: "All a job is good for is paying the bills." My friend confided in me one day about his dad's influence on his work philosophy. It led my buddy to bounce around from job to job, switching career paths numerous times.

MEN CHOOSE TO BE UNDERCHALLENGED

I am typing this section from a café. I love coming here because the coffee is good, the food is even better, and the environment is creative. For years I have done my work here, and I always end up talking to interesting people.

Today I had a conversation with one of the regulars. He is in his forties and lives near the café. He is quite versed in current affairs and seems to be intelligent. In getting to know him, I discovered that he has had a string of jobs. He has managed a bar and grill, taught piano lessons, and walked dogs for wealthy people. There is nothing wrong with managing and teaching. There is also nothing wrong with walking dogs, unless the dogs weigh under ten pounds. There *is* something wrong with my friend not maximizing his God-given potential. He has a brilliant mind but lazy hands. His heart is content with living beneath his masculinity. He has quieted his internal hard wiring to attain work that is commensurate with his talents. He is coasting, and it is no surprise that he is single.

In one of our many conversations he revealed that he refuses to be stressed. He wants a life that he can manage, a life that is under his control. He doesn't want to work for anyone, and he doesn't really want to risk starting a business. He refuses any challenges and likes it that way.

MEN INAPPROPRIATELY LEAN ON THEIR WIVES TO PROVIDE

Something that came out in my counseling relationship with Jason and Rebecca was Jason's philosophy of choosing a mate. He had several dating relationships that could have culminated in marriage. I asked why he never pulled the trigger and proposed. He said, "Because none of these women were going to be successful." When I probed him about this, he acknowledged that this characteristic was high on his list for a spouse. In and of itself, desiring that your future spouse has income potential isn't a bad thing. But feminists are leading the way in showing us that when men fail to maximize their earning capacity because of their wives' incomes, their wives become resentful. The greater the financial burden a wife feels, the greater the potential for bitterness. These feelings occur in part because working women are still doing most of the household chores. When husbands don't take their roles as providers seriously, many wives feel that they are bearing a double burden.[5]

When husbands don't take their roles as providers seriously, many wives feel that they are bearing a double burden.

An old friend married his wife after a whirlwind engagement. They just celebrated twelve years of marriage. To say my friend is a free spirit is an understatement. He has had twenty-five jobs in the twenty years that I have known him. That tendency was partly what attracted Kristy to him. He was always up for something new, and their marriage had a sense of adventure. But his chronic job hunt has worn on Kristy. In recent days, she told him that she has lost almost all respect for him because he isn't taking the role of being a provider seriously. She is tired of "bringing home most of the bacon" and longs for her husband to step up and stop living beneath his income potential.

As I have talked to hundreds of couples over the years, I have noticed resentment from wives in this area. It isn't just slacker husbands like this friend. Sometimes wives are frustrated with husbands who are stuck in middle management or are too comfortable with their companies. Wives love it when their husbands maximize their potential with regard to employment. It is more than a money issue. If a wife believes that her husband will lean into his role as provider, she is fueled to trust him with her (financial) future.

A BRIEF HISTORY OF WORK

Work did not begin as a separate sphere of life. According to anthropologists, it was essential for the survival of the hunter-gatherers. They didn't recognize the search for food as work. It was an urgent, daily need. It was about making it through the day rather than accruing some future benefit. As agricultural methods were discovered, civilizations developed, and so did the awareness of work as work. The first farmers sowed and tilled, knowing they would reap a crop in the future. As the production and storage of food advanced, civilizations became more sophisticated, leading to the rise of skilled specialists. With this new skilled labor, the notion of a job arose as these laborers were able to opt out of the all-consuming task of food production. They traded their skills for the chance to live off the surplus of others' work. The growing complexity and efficiency of food production promoted the increase of specialists, who were disconnected from the anxiety of the agricultural process. Abundance made it possible not to work every day. It made it possible to look forward to a relaxing weekend.

You would think in this evolution of work that a husband would rejoice in his job for the fact alone that he can rest from it. But many men don't rest well because they don't work that hard. They live for the weekend (working to rest well) instead of working from the weekend (resting to work well). They fail to find joy in the new work order that enables humans to work hard and live off the hard work of others.[6]

A THEOLOGY OF PROVIDING

What keeps husbands from getting joy from working hard and providing well? Although we could debate the new work order and its effects on men,[7] we need to talk about the original work order to figure out why husbands are struggling with provision.

The Bible tells us that work was part of God's good plan for creation from the beginning. There was a point when Murphy's Law did not wreak havoc on our work. It was an essential aspect of how Adam and Eve, the first humans, would participate in God's creation. Twice, the creation account in Genesis tells us that God created the garden of Eden and then placed the man there to "work it and keep it" (2:8, 15).

Early on, God had a specific calling for mankind: "God blessed them. And God said to them, 'Be fruitful and multiply and fill the earth and subdue it, and have dominion over the fish of the sea and over the birds of the heavens and over every living thing that moves on the earth'" (Gen. 1:28). The command was given to Adam and his wife, Eve. God commanded both to exercise dominion over the earth. That is, they were to exercise righteous rule over God's creation with God's authority. Women as well as men share in this authority and responsibility.

Herein lies an extraordinary vision for life. God does the heavy lifting by giving man the raw materials of nature. Then man gets to work with strength given by God to make something better. God creates, and man cultivates God's good creation. The command from God to his first son tells us something about what it means to be a provider. We are to work our version of the garden and keep it. Nature was made to be tended by skilled cultivators. The garden of Eden was good, but it was in need of Adam's care.

To be a husband is to cultivate the soil of your wife's heart, drawing out and contributing to her beauty and goodness.

As God's ordained caretakers, we, too, have a duty toward the land. We can leave it lying there, untouched and uncultivated. Or we can bring out the best of it, "tending the garden and contributing to the world's goodness."[8] The same goes for our wives. The Old Norse word *husband* literally means "one who cultivates and prepares the soil." To be a husband is to cultivate the soil of your wife's heart, drawing out and contributing to her beauty and goodness.[9] Husbands are cultivators.

CULTIVATING IS NOT DAYDREAMING

My dad, who remains the hardest worker I've ever seen, would not like the word *cultivate*. He would prefer the word *work*. His argument would be that people who work produce, and people who cultivate dream. He has a point, but true cultivation results in production. To cultivate is to make the potential actual. One who cultivates is one who takes what is there and makes it better. He doesn't just have vision that isn't actionable. He isn't a legend in his own mind. He acts on his dreams and produces something good for the world.

CULTIVATING IS NOT EASY

Throughout the last decade I have done career counseling. I have talked to hundreds of young adults about what they feel called to do vocationally. *Warning*: I am going to sound like an old man lamenting the attitude of young whippersnappers. My experience has shown me that emerging generations are losing the work ethic that has caused culture to progress since the beginning of time.

I am encouraged that younger adults are so interested in natural foods. Many have gardens, and some are farming in urban areas.[10] Gardening is hard work because you can't do it successfully without weeding. You have to sort out what does and does not belong, what will bear fruit and what will choke it out. Andy Crouch, author of *Culture Making* and executive editor of *Christianity Today*, wrote, "The best creativity involves discarding that which is less than best, making room for the cultural goods that are the very best we can do with the world that has been given to us."[11]

Because providing is hard, men have to draw on resources beyond themselves. It is good for a man to realize that he is not God. It is also good for a man to bring out the full potential of his job in a way that magnifies his coworkers and the values of his business. When a man embraces his God-given call to cultivate, he experiences delight in his work. He begins to understand that his past has prepared him to be where he is vocationally. He starts to embrace the present and devotes himself fully to maximizing the employment opportunity that is before him. He gets a vision for his legacy in the future.

WHY DON'T MEN EMBRACE THE ROLE OF PROVIDER?

What we see in the garden is that Adam and Eve chose to be consumers rather than cultivators. The commission they received from God—to be fruitful, multiply, and fill the earth—meant they needed to fix their eyes on the uncultivated land beyond Eden. They needed to trust God's goodness and plan. The temptation from Satan took the form of an invitation to consume rather than cultivate.[12] And so they turned their gaze inward, to the tree in the midst of the garden—the very one that God had forbidden to them. God had given them the freedom to eat of every tree of the perfect garden, and they chose that one because they could.

If both Adam and Eve disobeyed God—and Eve started it—why am I pressing in on the husbands here? And what's this got to do with a man's workplace?

First, the Bible is clear that even though Eve was responsible for taking the fruit (sinning first), Adam was held accountable as the head of the marriage (more on this in chapter 8, "Submit").[13] He was supposed to protect and guide his wife, but he failed to do either one.

Second, the creation account seems to suggest that although both Adam and Eve were called to cultivate God's good creation, they were given distinctive roles in the process. Eve's very name means "mother of all living" (Gen. 3:20). Like Eve, wives have a unique call to carry babies in their bodies and feed babies from their bodies. Like Adam, husbands seem to have an intrinsic and unique call to lead in providing financially for their families.[14]

Like Adam, husbands seem to have an intrinsic and unique call to lead in providing financially for their families.

We see this in the way that consequences fell uniquely

upon the woman and the man. The Bible calls these consequences "curses," and they are as follows:

The curse on the woman (Gen. 3:16):

To the woman he said,
"I will surely multiply your pain in childbearing;
in pain you shall bring forth children.
Your desire shall be for your husband,
and he shall rule over you."

The curse on the man (3:17–19):

And to Adam he said,
"Because you have listened to the voice of your wife
and have eaten of the tree
of which I commanded you,
'You shall not eat of it,'
cursed is the ground because of you;
in pain you shall eat of it all the days of your life;
thorns and thistles it shall bring forth for you;
and you shall eat the plants of the field.
By the sweat of your face
you shall eat bread,
till you return to the ground,
for out of it you were taken;
for you are dust,
and to dust you shall return."

The curse on the woman is related not just to the pain in childbirth. Some theologians think that this idea of pain in childbirth is a metaphor for the reality that women tend to be more homeward in their orientation than their husbands.[15] There are exceptions, but social science seems to confirm what the ancient wisdom of the Bible explains: the woman's curse is found in the thing in which she has unique gifts to be a leader.

The curse for the husband is on the work of his hands. This verse seems to foreshadow Murphy's Law. Although we might think the whole sweat thing is about hard manual labor, it's likely an ancient Near Eastern idiom referring to "anxiety" and "perspiration-inducing fear."[16] The curse is not work itself, but the limitation of resources and an insecure future in a world that no longer responds to our commands. The implication of this curse is that the ground's rebellion against man serves as a reminder of man's rebellion against his Creator. The curse of sin comes on God's unique calling for a husband.

As I said in *The Dude's Guide to Manhood*:

> A man's temptation is either to hate his job or love it too much—to demonize or idolize it. He either begrudges the work and avoids it or allows it to become his master. But a truly free man knows the limits of his work. He is not free from work, but free to work well. The work serves him and brings out the best in him, rather than destroying him or taking over.[17]

WISDOM FROM MY WIFE

Over the course of our marriage, Darrin and I have lived out several scenarios regarding work, providing financially for our family, and managing our home. Different seasons of life required different adjustments. When we were newly married, both of us were going to school and working part-time, and we split household responsibilities down the middle. Later, I served as the primary breadwinner while Darrin crammed three years of grad school into two and worked as an unpaid intern, and we got everything else done as best we could. Shortly after that, we both worked full-time for several years before our first child was born. I then worked part-time from home while Darrin continued working full-time, and we were fortunate to be able to coordinate a schedule that allowed us to take turns caring for our daughter every day.

We moved to a new city and realized quickly that Darrin's job was going to be extremely stressful and time consuming. Having a peaceful home environment was important, but it wasn't going to happen without planning and management. We knew that being involved in a start-up was going to require a lot of unpaid work and support from me as well. Our strong desire was for our then one-year-old daughter to be able to spend the majority of her time with us. Although it was a risky decision that required financial sacrifices, I feel extremely fortunate that we were able to make it work at all. Many couples and parents don't have much of a choice in this matter. I am thankful every day for this tremendous privilege, and I always want to be mindful and intentional of stewarding our options well.

As we've added three more children to our family and as our church and ministry responsibilities have grown considerably, I have continued to work mainly at home, and Darrin has taken primary responsibility for providing financially for our family. Again, we based this decision on our values, our circumstances, and our desire to provide for our family on physical, emotional, spiritual, and mental levels.

Our decision is more about the type of work each of us will do and who takes primary leadership in specific areas. I lead in managing our home. Darrin is involved in daily household tasks, but I take responsibility for how household tasks will get done and who does what. Darrin submits to my leadership in this area. I am in charge of our children's daily schedules, but Darrin and I parent every day on practical and deeper, more emotional and spiritual levels. Darrin takes primary responsibility for providing financially for our family, but as my other responsibilities allow, I help with this, and we collaborate on financial decisions and planning.

We felt that each of us owning specific areas of leadership was the wisest decision so that both of us weren't spread thin over several areas of necessary and important work. In the future, as our children get older and our situation changes, it's likely that I will provide much more significantly on a financial level and that other aspects of who does what will change dramatically.

I have never viewed my work as any less important than Darrin's work as the primary breadwinner. He has never treated me as less important or influential in our family because he makes more money. And our decisions in these areas have never been about a lack of intelligence, capability, or ambition on my part. Darrin has been my biggest cheerleader in encouraging me to use my talents and abilities inside and outside our home, and he has made sacrifices so that I have had opportunities to do so.

These decisions can be complicated, and sometimes our choices are limited and may require us to be creative and work through various steps over time to reach the bigger goal. There's not just one right way to prioritize home and family while providing for a family. But husbands, committing to the work of being a provider and cultivator is absolutely worth the effort. Your wisdom and commitment in this area can bring peace and freedom to your wives and families.

Five Good Questions

1. Do you feel that I'm committed to providing for our family?
2. What do you see me cultivating on a regular basis?
3. Are there areas in which I lean too heavily on your capability and neglect my responsibility?
4. Do you feel that I have a healthy and biblical perspective on work?
5. How do our current roles and responsibilities fit into our values regarding work and providing for our family?

CHAPTER 6

REST

A rested husband is a peaceful husband.

I STARTED OUR CHURCH, THE JOURNEY, WITH THREE PEO-ple including myself. My wife and one-year-old daughter were the other two. You've already heard Amie mention my eighty-hour workweeks during the first few years. Recruiting new members, counseling current ones, and teaching anyone who would hear me occupied my waking hours. I slept about four hours a night and took only a handful of days off for five years.

Overwork and lack of rest are attractive because they produce results. The church grew from three to thirteen hundred, and we started four more churches in five years. I was asked to speak at conferences around the world, and multiple pastors wanted coaching from me to learn the recipe for the secret sauce. The truth is that the recipe was the unsustainable combination of working all the time and resting very little. This deadly pattern hurt my marriage and children in profound ways.

Right at the end of this craziness, my son was heading into his toddler years. I was attempting to work less and rest more as he was beginning to walk. I was trying to teach my little boy how to pace himself. He went one hundred miles per hour most of the day and then crashed around dinner, sometimes falling asleep face-first in his plate. So I told him he needed to take a nap; he should go to his room and rest. I assumed that when he went to his room, he slept. You know what they say about people who assume. Drew wasn't sleeping; he was playing quietly.

The culture in which we live seems to have forgotten the need for sabbath. And it is killing us and our marriages!

I realized that if Drew was going to rest, I was going to have to show him how. I scooped up my little guy, took him into my bedroom, and napped with him. In doing so I was acting like God: "On the seventh day God finished his work that he had done, and he rested on the seventh day from all his work that he had done" (Gen. 2:2).

Even people who are familiar with the Bible may know little about the principle of sabbath, especially its practice. Religious or nonreligious, the culture in which we live seems to have forgotten the need for sabbath. And it is killing us and our marriages! Without rest, you have no patience to listen and no desire to talk. The fights never resolve, and you grow bitter.

It's been more than two decades since Juliet Schor's *The Overworked American* was published, but the trends she observed in her research do not appear to be slowing down at all.[1] Just read these statistics from the American Psychological Association:

- In 2001, the median number of days away from work as a result of anxiety, stress, and related disorders was twenty-five—substantially greater than the median of six for all nonfatal injury and illness cases.
- Job stress is estimated to cost U.S. industry more than $300 billion a year in absenteeism, turnover, diminished productivity, and medical, legal, and insurance costs.
- Eighteen percent of U.S. workers put in more than forty-eight hours a week.
- Eighty-three percent of employees report going to work even while sick, citing heavy workload, need to conserve time off to meet family needs, and a work environment where taking off is "risky" as their rationale.

And that's just a fraction of the statistics the association compiled on a Psychologically Healthy Workplace Program's Fact Sheet in 2013.[2]

I mention Schor's work because there's certainly an American flavor to overwork and burnout. It's not as if people in other countries are immune to the issue, but we can learn a lot from them, especially Europeans. The United States is the only nation in a group of twenty-one that does not require employers to provide paid vacation, as reported by the Center for Economic and Policy Research.[3] Granted there are significant economic differences to consider, but as Americans, we can stand to learn how to unplug during off-hours and work smarter. Several European countries are even making significant strides with on-the-job education and subsidized child care.[4]

However, rest isn't simply physical; it is also spiritual. What would it look like to take off one day a week? What would it be like to look forward to that day as a time that would empower the other six days? What would it look like to be fully engaged in that day? What would it look like to enter the workweek having been filled spiritually, relationally, and emotionally?

IMITATING GOD IN REST

Okay, back to the Bible for ancient wisdom. The Genesis account of creation teaches us several things about how we can imitate God in rest. We can imitate God by doing good work, not being hurried in our work, actually ceasing from our work, and then celebrating our work.

WE DO GOOD WORK

The biblical narrative tells us that God was quite busy for six days. He created both the visible and the invisible worlds. If you have traveled much or at least have watched the National Geographic channel, you know that God did pretty well.[5]

One reason we don't rest well is that we don't work hard. Sociologists have been throwing around the concept of weisure a lot in the past few years.[6] *Weisure*, the blurring of work and leisure, was directed at the encroachment of work into rest. Our increased accessibility through smartphones and tablets has expanded our office space. But it's also enabling us to take our play into work with us, distracting us from our necessary tasks.

Husbands, you have to look at yourself in the mirror on this one. Let me give you some questions to consider:

Am I giving my best at work?

Is my employer (if I work for someone else), or my dream (if I work for myself), being served well? Am I giving my attention and energy to my job?

Am I giving my best at home?

Does my wife believe that I am all in for her? Does she feel my affection? Would she say that I am attentive to her? When I am, do I give her the focus that she deserves? Do I know the hearts—not just the actions—of my children? Do

I know my kids' friends, not just their names? Would my children say they have my undivided attention?

WE REFUSE TO BE HURRIED IN OUR WORK

It is impossible to rest well when you are rushed. One part of Christian theology I love is that God is revealed as one who is never in a hurry.[7] Maybe part of how to tap into rest is to approach life without hurry.

Years ago, I was listening to one of my spiritual heroes, John Ortberg. He was talking about a time when he spent one hour with one of his spiritual heroes, Dallas Willard. He came up with a question to ask his mentor, thinking, *I'm going to ask this question and then let him talk for like an hour.* The question was this: "How can I deepen my relationship with God?" How can I really know God? How can I really experience God? That's the heart of the question. With his pen and paper ready, he asked the question, and his mentor responded, "You must ruthlessly eliminate hurry from your life." Full stop. John waited for more information, but his mentor just looked at him in silence. The mentoring session was over.[8]

Hurry is dangerous, if not toxic, to resting well. If your whole week is a flurry of activity devoid of rest, you will approach the sabbath the same way. If I am frantic all week, I use most of my sabbath detoxing instead of refreshing. Many of us live frantic lives, full of multitasking, clutter, and relational shallowness. We feel dominated by life. We run from one thing to another in this sleep-deprived state bolstered only by caffeine, sugar, and the constant stimulus from our dumb smartphones. This causes us to be unthoughtful and unimaginative in our jobs.[9] God has given us an opportunity to weave rest, which is the opposite of hurriedness, into the fabric of our schedules and our very souls.

WE SHOULD CEASE FROM OUR WORK

You know how hard this is if you have ever been involved in a start-up. I remember when I started the church. I felt as though the world would stop if I stopped. I was convinced that "if it is going to be, it is up to me." Many of my coaches and professors flat-out said that if I wasn't working seventy to eighty hours, I wasn't really doing my job. I question that wisdom now. I question it philosophically because of my spirituality and practically because of my physicality. I set in place bad patterns in my spiritual life during this time that have been tough to shake. I still suffer the bodily consequences of overwork.

Hurry is dangerous, if not toxic, to resting well.

My counselor has really challenged the *why* of my overwork. We have had many conversations, but here is the gist of why I work too hard and rest too poorly: *I think I'm God*. Sabbath is God's way of dethroning us. Sabbath is God's way of reminding us of our creatureliness. Sabbath humbles us by telling us, "You do not have endless energy. You are not invincible. You may not go on forever in your own strength. You may not run at four thousand rpms." Sabbath is God's way of showing us we're not God. Yet it's also God's way of dignifying us.

WE SHOULD CELEBRATE OUR WORK

The order of events is important. God worked six days, and he rested on the seventh. Then after the rest, God began to rule over what he created. It seems that God's reign over his creation involved a celebration of that creation. Theologian Sandra Richter said that in the ancient Near East, rest "was something that conquering kings had and did when their enemies were defeated and their domain was fully under their control . . . a king who had proven himself a king 'rested.'"[10] This is the very image of God: "enthroned above his peaceful and productive domain."[11] Through the sabbath, God invites us into his rest.

WHAT DO I DO ON THE SABBATH?

When you observe the Sabbath, you cease from what is duty. Now I'm not saying that you tell the kids to make their own mac and cheese. I'm not saying that you ignore some of your responsibilities. I am saying that you don't do things you don't have to do.

DON'T DO WHAT YOU DON'T HAVE TO DO

This is the day you don't do laundry. This is the day you don't go to the store. This is the day you don't do anything that's not absolutely urgent. Sabbath is about breaking routine. My wife and I hate doing house chores. Washing dishes, sweeping, vacuuming, doing laundry, and wiping down counters often feel like soul-crushing tasks. On the sabbath we avoid this daily maintenance. We structure our week to get these things done ahead of time. We empower our kids to fend for themselves in age-appropriate ways.

But Sabbath is about more. It's active. You engage in things that bring you life and give you joy. Sabbath includes play. It's about good food and drink. It's about family and friends.

DO TRY TO CONNECT WITH GOD

This is a day of worship. Yes, it's rest, but it's also remembrance. Sabbath is about remembering what is truly life by forgetting normal life for a day. Jews and Christians give special attention to God. We put away the distractions and set our gaze on God. This day is about knowing God more deeply.

Sabbath is about remembering what is truly life by forgetting normal life for a day.

Mark Buchanan is a gifted writer on these truths. He said, "Some knowing is never pursued, only received."[12] Some things you can know only if you're receiving, not pursuing. What is that kind of knowing? What is that goal? It's not just taking a Sabbath day. The goal is to have a Sabbath heart. It's not just a day of rest but a heart of rest. It's not just a day of focus but a heart that is rightfully focused. There is a pulling back.

There is a passive element, but it's active as well. There is a pressing in.

DO THINGS THAT REFRESH YOUR SOUL

Among the things I love about Christian theology is the concept of grace. Grace says that I can rest from my work because my significance, my meaning, and my identity do not come from what I do. I don't have to go frantically from one thing to another in my life. The ultimate person in the universe is already impressed not because of my work but because of the work of Jesus Christ, the embodiment of grace. Sabbath rest reminds me that the work has already been done by a perfect man who loves me in my imperfection.

Because I don't have to perform for God, trying to earn his favor, I can delight in his world. I can bask in the creativity of God by going outside to enjoy nature, whether it is going to a park or sitting on my deck. Even doing yard work helps me connect to God and celebrate the goodness of his work.

DO GET AWAY FROM MEDIA

I read about a Detroit newspaper that offered $500 to 120 families if they would refrain from watching TV for a month as part of a marketing deal. What's interesting is that 93 of the 120 turned down the offer. But the 27 who accepted reported that it was a life-changing decision for their families.[13]

Not a big TV watcher? How about video games? Movies?

YouTube? Whatever media you need to turn off, turn it off. Get away from your phone. You may experience PPV all the time. It sounds like a venereal disease, but it stands for phantom phone vibration. Your leg starts vibrating, and you think it's your phone, but it's not there.

Your body is responding to something that's not there because your phone is always buzzing. What if you got away from your phone? I know you like your smartphone, but it distracts you from what is most important.

DO BE INTIMATE WITH YOUR WIFE

Some sects of Judaism literally said you should have sex four times on the Sabbath.[14] My wife thinks that's extreme. But this is the time, couples, for you to connect physically without the burden and hurry of the world. Enjoy each other physically. I am not just talking about sex. Stay in bed longer in the morning. Don't be rushed. Just lie there and talk.

When Amie and I go on vacation, we certainly love the beach or the mountains or the city that is our destination. We love new activities and new places. But the best part is just hanging out in our room, talking, reading, and watching TV. The marriage bed is all about intimacy.[15] Sometimes that involves sex; sometimes it doesn't.

DON'T BE RUSHED

Just relax. Practice slowing down. Drive in the slow lane, as much as it kills you. Stand in the long line at the grocery store. Chew your food at least ten times before you swallow.

Think of other ways to slow down. Then I encourage you to celebrate. God did this. Here is the pattern: God acted, he stepped back, and he celebrated what he had created and what he did.

See, here's the thing, friends. If you don't choose the sabbath, the sabbath will choose you, and the results will be illness, burnout, and relational brokenness.

Hear from Amie now on how my brokenness in this area hurt our marriage:

When Darrin feels out of control or doesn't know what to do, he defaults to work. It took me several years to put this together, but I eventually started to see the connection between Darrin's failure to rest and seasons in our church or our family when it felt as if there were insurmountable obstacles. Darrin spent more hours in his office or on his phone instead of resting or pursuing healthy recreation. Anxious, "I don't know what to do" conversations were followed by more work, not rest.

If you don't choose the sabbath, the sabbath will choose you, and the results will be illness, burnout, and relational brokenness.

If he was too exhausted to work, he tried to put other people, including our family, to work. If Darrin walked in the door and the house seemed messy or chaotic, sometimes his first reaction was to angrily ask our kids to clean something up or get to work in another way. It didn't matter what they were doing at the moment and that they had already done something helpful that day. This approach rarely produced the desired result.

During a particularly stressful season, we both noticed that our kids were disappearing into their rooms whenever Darrin came home. Their behavior obviously concerned us. We eventually realized that when Darrin felt things were out of his control, he tried to make himself feel better by asking the kids to control the home environment (pick up, clean up) for him.

We had several difficult conversations about this because he could not see the connection immediately. I had to be persistent and not just cave in to the easy fix of doing what Darrin asked in order to ease his tension temporarily. Asking your kids to be responsible for their belongings and messes and to be helpful in the context of working together as a family is desirable and an important goal. But Darrin's demanding requests were more about him trying to make himself feel better than they were about promoting the good of the family and contributing to peace in our home. Ultimately, his actions didn't produce lasting peace for him, and the kids felt used.

There will always be more work to do. Work is a terrible replacement for rest. Waiting until all the work is finished to rest means that rest will never happen. We have to plan for it and choose to follow through on those plans. The need for rest is a legitimate part of our humanness, and there's humility in cooperating with our God-given limits.

Seeing Darrin make disciplined choices to work hard

and rest well helps me trust his leadership for our family. Because I know that overworking is a way that Darrin tries to avoid God, I feel less secure and cared for when he operates from that desperate, "gotta-make-it-happen" mentality. I feel more free to rest when I see Darrin making rest a priority for himself. Darrin's constant push to work placed an unvoiced expectation on me and our family that rest was a last resort, not a part of our regular routine.

Even though I value rest and refreshment, it felt like swimming upstream to take healthy breaks when the general vibe all around me was to push through, no matter what. I'm absolutely responsible for myself when it comes to prioritizing rest, but the mixed messages that Darrin was sending through the way he was living definitely didn't help me live from those beliefs.

There's a big difference between laziness, inertia, mindlessness, and a disciplined choice to rest. Disciplined rest is restorative; the other options are draining. We act out of what we truly believe. If we don't believe in the importance and value of rest, we won't do it.

Amie just confirmed an important truth: a rested husband is an enjoyable husband. Tired people are cranky or distracted or both. No one enjoys cranky, distracted people. Being rested helps a man control his emotions and give loved ones appropriate attention.[16] When you are tired, you're in a survival mode. You lack the energy to engage nature or the deeper issues of life. It's hard to become too emotionally involved with anyone, especially your wife. You can barely hold up your head, much less care about what's going on with your spouse. But a rested husband is a thoughtful husband. He taps into a bigger world and engages his wife's heart.

Five Good Questions

1. Do you think that I rest well? Why or why not?
2. How am I different when I'm rested and when I'm not?
3. How can we cultivate a healthy view of rest and refreshment in our family?
4. Do you see me habitually engaging in any mindless activities that I could replace with a more refreshing activity?
5. Are there ways that you see me trying to avoid rest?

CHAPTER 7

SERVE

To love is bliss; to serve is divine.

—Unknown

I GREW UP IN THE 1970S WHEN THE PROTOTYPE FOR fatherhood was Archie Bunker, the protagonist in the sitcom *All in the Family.* A product of the Great Depression, Archie was raised in poverty, and his childhood was marked by the taunts of other children who always seemed to have more. He was a gifted baseball player with a dream to play for the Yankees, but he had to give it up to support his family. He worked the docks after serving in World War II and seemed to embody the phrase "blue collar." With his broken dreams and long-winded diatribes, Archie tapped into the nation's consciousness like few other characters from that or any other era. He most frequently appeared resting in a brown tweed chair in his living room, a beer in hand, his wife scurrying about to satisfy his every whim after a hard day's work. Today, that wingback chair, with its stained armrests and frayed upholstery, sits in the National Museum of American History.

I don't know whether life imitates art or art imitates life. But my home was a lot like Archie's. So were my friends' homes. We received the message that inside the home a wife's job was to serve her husband, not the other way around. Husbands worked, and wives served. No idea could be more damaging to a marriage.

My college hero was the anti–Archie Bunker. Recently, I built a friendship with this hero, an author who deeply influenced my life when I was in college. My college years were a time of deep learning for me, not just about my major but about myself. The words from this man helped me work through deep pain in my life and helped set the trajectory for all that I am doing in my career.

I met my hero because his son started attending our church. I was able to have lunch with him and ask him all kinds of questions. This happened once every couple of years, culminating with a three-hour Q&A he did for some of our staff. It was an amazing night. From there, my hero left with his wife to lead a retreat in another state. Shortly after they arrived, his wife collapsed from a stroke and fell into a multi-month coma.

My hero became my hero again as he faithfully wrote about his new life with his ailing wife every day as she recovered. I eagerly read these updates to see how she was doing and how he was coping. He did not hide his pain or frustration. His writing was at times eloquent and at other times raw. But the tenor of his posts was summed up one day when he said, "With [my wife] unable to do anything for herself, I am back in the place I should have always been, her servant." Mind blown.

My first jobs were in service industries. In my landscaping job I was a one-man show who mowed yards in a fairly mediocre manner. I had three clients, who fired me abruptly. Then I became a busboy in a local steak house. I worked for minimum wage, which at the time was less than the amount for any drink you can buy today at Starbucks. My job was to assist the waitstaff so that they could focus on serving customers. I was paid to serve the servers who made tons of money via tips. This inequity made me angry. I decided that I should have some of the tips, so occasionally I borrowed money left on the table. When the boss found out, I was quickly terminated.

I am not good at serving. I would much rather be served. Many husbands can relate.

WHY HUSBANDS DON'T SERVE THEIR WIVES

Maybe your dad wasn't Archie Bunker, but he probably didn't provide a good example of how to serve one's wife. Serving our wives even if we did have a good model is tough. Why is this?

BEING IGNORANT OF HOW YOUR WIFE LIKES TO BE SERVED

Years ago when Amie and I were newly married, we attended a marriage seminar that discussed Gary Chapman's ideas regarding love languages.[1] Over twelve years of counseling couples, he worked to discover what each spouse desired in order to be loved. It became clear that what makes one person feel loved does not necessarily make another person feel loved. After reviewing his extensive notes, he found that the responses given to the question generally fell into five categories:

1. words of affirmation = vocal encouragement
2. quality time = giving the other person your undivided attention
3. giving gifts = giving thoughtfully chosen gifts on a regular basis
4. acts of service = actions speak louder than words
5. physical touch = nothing speaks more deeply than appropriate touch[2]

My wife's primary love language is gifts, which was awesome because we were newlyweds when we heard Chapman for the first time. We could barely afford our rent and ramen noodles. "Baby, here is a gift . . . I made Hamburger Helper with real hamburger this time!" My primary love language is acts of service, which fit right in with my philosophy of being served without having to serve. It didn't take too many years of marriage for me to see that I had a deficient philosophy that would destroy my marriage if I did not repent of it. For more on the love languages, see appendix D.

BEING EXHAUSTED

When you are tired, you want to be served and then left alone. For several years I had chronic fatigue. The only way to describe being under the spell of this disease is that I felt like a zombie. I woke up from a good night's sleep and felt as if I didn't sleep a wink. I had to drink multiple cups of coffee in the afternoon just to make it through the day. I would have a few good days and usually good parts of every day. But when the fatigue hit, I was undone.

> It didn't take too many years of marriage for me to see that I had a deficient philosophy that would destroy my marriage if I did not repent of it.

Justifying a lack of serving with being tired is easy. Husband, you may not have chronic fatigue, but if you are working and providing for your family physically, emotionally, and spiritually, you are tired. For years, I chose to spend my limited energy and overfocus on my job. This meant my wife and kids got the short end of the service stick. Yes, my energy was limited, but if I'm honest, I could have chosen to short other areas of my life instead.

NOT DEALING WITH STRESS

A physician concluded in the 1950s, "Stress in addition to being itself, was also the cause of itself, and the result of itself."[3] *Stress* can seem like an umbrella term to describe our entire lives. But can we be specific? At its basic level, stress is the response of the body to any demand for change. Stress can be either good or bad; it depends on the duration. When something triggers this response, our fight-or-flight mechanism is engaged. Nerve chemicals and hormones are released so we can flee to safety or face the threat. Once the danger passes, the body restores itself to normal functioning. But when stress becomes chronic, the same chemicals and hormones that were helpful in short bursts remain, preventing your body from resetting and relaxing. The psychological aspect of chronic stress creates an overreactive fight-or-flight response within us. We view every demand as a threat and constantly look for potential threats.[4]

Understanding what is going on inside you is the starting point. If you are going to respond properly to stress, you need to recognize how it plays out in various arenas. Psychologists have recently started using the terms *spillover* and *crossover* to describe work-family stress.[5] Spillover occurs when a man's stress at work leads to a man's stress at home. Crossover occurs when a man's stress at work leads to a wife's stress at home. You can transfer your stress not just from one location to the next but also onto your spouse.

I was raised near a lake that had a spillover—a place to house and disperse water when it got too high for the banks and dam. The spillover was about two hundred feet long and four hundred feet deep. It absorbed thousands of gallons of water to keep the lake at equilibrium. When we don't have good outlets for stress, our wives and children become our spillovers. They did not sign up for that job. And when you're taking on that much pressure, the amount added to the equation seems unbearable.

One way to reduce the spillover is to have some bridge activity that helps you disengage from the grind and reengage your family. It could be listening to a podcast, exercising, doing light yard work, or even watching a TV show. There are only a couple of rules: Tell your spouse about your intentions with the activity, and make sure it doesn't take up the entire evening. Otherwise you defeat the purpose.

NOT SWITCHING HATS

As I've served as the chaplain to the St. Louis Cardinals over the last few years, I have discovered many unknown servants working behind the scenes of the stadium. People tirelessly take care of the operations and details so the players can focus on playing the game they love. At the front of the line of these unsung heroes are the clubbies. Clubbies, in short, serve the players. They do their laundry, set reservations, manage ticket requests, and clean up after them.

You may not have a clubbie, but maybe you have an assistant and perhaps a few direct reports. You may be the boss and spend the day giving directives that must be followed. Or you may not manage anyone and spend the day being managed. Whether you spend your day being a boss or being bossed, you have to switch hats when you come through the door to greet your bride.

WHAT ARE SOME WAYS FOR HUSBANDS TO SERVE?

DO THINGS SHE DOESN'T LIKE TO DO

It's easy to serve in areas that you like or are easy for you. When Amie and I were first married, we lived in a series of small apartments. The first few didn't have a full-sized refrigerator, much less a dishwasher. I appointed myself the dishwasher, partly out of necessity (we had a small sink and no counter space to hold dirty dishes) and partly from genetics (my mom was a dishwashing machine). I took great pride in washing dishes. I was doing more than washing dishes; I was being a good husband. On the other hand, I hated doing laundry, and we had to go to the Laundromat to take care of that task. Amie abhorred doing it. The one time I went to do the laundry, I shrank a bunch of her sweaters. I was immediately demoted and quite relieved. I kept washing dishes and feeling justified in my service. I thought I was serving my wife, but I should have improved my laundry skills. Then I really would have been serving my wife. What your wife doesn't enjoy should be the focus of your service to her.

DON'T ASSUME, ASK

It is easy to think that your wife wants to be served the way you like to be served. Doing this may be a love language mistake. (See appendix D.) Don't just assume that you know what your wife needs or what seems to be service to her. If your wife isn't responding well to your service, there's a strong possibility that you're projecting ways that you would like to be served onto her. There's not a right or wrong here; it's just that different people prefer different kinds of help. She might not care less about your help with a house project, but she would love for you to run a random errand for her.

OWN YOUR AREA

Remember that fight Amie and I had over the clutter on the dresser? I just looked at my nightstand before I got up this morning. It is a haven for mess: a dozen books, various magazines, multiple water bottles, and more than a handful of protein bar wrappers. I went down to my desk in my home office, which was littered with coffee cups and pieces of paper. Then I got in my car to go to an appointment and found more water bottles, sunglasses, and books. It occurred to me that my wife experiences all my messes on a daily basis. A simple way to serve her is to clean up after myself. Whether it's the dishes, the nightstand, or your man cave or office, be a man and serve your wife well by picking up after yourself.[6]

ACKNOWLEDGE HER WORK

Your wife may have a highly stressful job. My friend's wife is a major player in a Fortune 500 company. They are juggling the demands of a growing family while both of them are growing their careers. To his credit, my friend acknowledges that his wife is going through a tough season and is doing good work. Yet research has found that breadwinning wives still do *at least two-thirds* of the housework.[7]

> Whether it's the dishes, the nightstand, or your man cave or office, be a man and serve your wife well by picking up after yourself.

Every husband thinks he is working hard until he has to watch the kids by himself. Never a truer statement has been uttered. I discovered this last month when I took all four kids for five days by myself. I came back in sackcloth and ashes, lauding my wife for the demanding job that is managing our home.

Failing to Recognize Your Wife's Superiority

Carin Rubenstein, author of *The Superior Wife Syndrome*, commented: "Husbands tend not to see how much more their wives do, or how much more their wives sacrifice, or how much more peeved and distressed their wives feel."[8] Husbands have a tendency to misinterpret, misreport, or misunderstand their wives' superiority. She lists four reasons why guys don't see it:

1. Men exaggerate. The issue is not lying. It's that most guys perceive themselves to be accomplish-

ing a lot. They're just wrong. "[Men] are domestic legends in their own mind: every time they move a single load of laundry to the dryer, they are doing all of the laundry," Rubenstein said. "Every time they read a bedtime story, they are always putting the children to sleep. Every time they scramble eggs on Sunday, they are cooking family meals. Indeed, men consistently overestimate their contributions at home in just about every study on the topic, including my own."[9]

2. Some men are deliberately obtuse. These guys pretend to be less capable than they are. "Honey, you're just better at it" becomes their excuse to avoid responsibility.
3. Some men are really and truly oblivious. If you are one of these guys, the next section is for you.
4. Some husbands feel threatened by their wives' superiority. If you are one of these guys, make sure you don't just skim the next chapter.

ASK HER!

Many of the paths to serving your wife I've mentioned thus far have been indirect—figuring out her love language, developing a bridge activity, owning your area. But perhaps the best route is the most direct one: just ask her what she needs.

Ask your wife what it feels like to be served. Is it easy or difficult for her to receive help? How did her family members serve one another (or not)? Connect with your wife's heart by learning what it *feels* like when you serve her, not just what she is able to check off her list because you served her.

Looking for ways to serve your wife is a discipline that you can practice on a daily basis, such as exercising, eating well, or managing time. Make it fun! Look for opportunities to surprise her. Don't point out what you've done; let her discover it and enjoy it on her own. True service has no strings attached, so don't make your help conditional or pout if you don't get the affirmation you'd prefer.

On behalf of all our wives who love being served, let Amie close out this chapter for us:

In our house, I coordinate the logistics of our lives. It's my job to keep things running smoothly. I especially feel cared for when Darrin takes ownership of some of the details around holidays and family vacations. It's great when he asks for feedback after he's served me and then applies it. These practical acts of service remind me that I exist and am loved for reasons other than just being useful and productive.

Five Good Questions

1. How did your family members serve one another when you were growing up?
2. Tell me about a time when someone served you well. What did that feel like?

3. How can we develop a culture of serving one another well in our family?
4. What are three practical ways I can serve you on a regular basis?
5. Is there a task you really dislike that I could do for you?

CHAPTER 8

SUBMIT

Selflessness is the soul of teamwork.

—Phil Jackson

MY WIFE IS BETTER AT A LOT OF THINGS THAN I AM. That is one reason I married her. I wanted to be challenged. I wanted to learn. I wanted to grow. I wanted a woman, not a robot. I got what I wanted and more. Amie is very smart. Her IQ is higher than mine. Her EI (emotional intelligence) is definitely higher than mine. I married up. I outpunted my coverage. I have a better half. Can I get a witness?

Not every man wants a wife like mine. Steve, the dad of one of my high school friends, said he intentionally married beneath himself so he could do "what I darned well please." His wife's chief virtue was kindness, not confidence.

She lacked the verbal skill to stand up to her husband, so he dominated her, just as he wanted to do.

Steve couldn't stand not being in control. At his job, he demanded that employees comply with his orders and carry them out exactly as he wanted. In his parenting, he berated his children with an angry cliché: "My way or the highway." My friend often opted for the highway (also known as my couch).

Most of us immediately cringe when we think about that dad. There's no gentleness, no tenderness. As Westerners living in the twenty-first century, we can easily recognize deficiencies in his character. A couple of millennia ago, those defects would not have been so apparent. Many of our contemporary assumptions about character are rooted in classical society. But, none of the ancient philosophers, such as Plato and Aristotle, spoke of humility and gentleness as marks of good character. Submission was not a virtue in the Greco-Roman world. A willingness to yield, to defer to another, was considered slave behavior.

The early Christians honored submission as a cultural value. You may have heard this famous line uttered from Jesus' lips: "The last will be first, and the first last" (Matt. 20:16). That was such a revolutionary idea that even the disciples who were with him the most didn't get it. The mom of two of them, James and John, asked Jesus if her sons could sit on either side of his throne. The other ten overheard the conversation and became indignant.

Jesus ended their bickering not by softening his stance but by making it even more difficult to accept. "Whoever would be great among you must be your servant," he said, "and whoever would be first among you must be your slave" (Matt. 20:26–27). Jesus entirely reframed the rules of their competition. He exposed their conflict for what it was—pride.

Jesus handpicked these guys. He gave more of his time and teaching to them than to others. Yet the thought of others enjoying more access than they had made them livid. And that's really the root of pride: being offended at the mere thought of someone else having more power and control. Few have articulated this idea better than C. S. Lewis, who wrote, "Pride gets no pleasure out of having something, only out of having more of it than the next [person]." You may think you're proud of being successful, intelligent, or good-looking. But when you are surrounded by those who are equal or better than you in these things, you lose all pleasure. "It is the comparison that makes you proud: the pleasure of being above the rest."[1]

"Pride gets no pleasure of having something, only out of having it more than the next [person]."

Pride lurks in the heart of every human being. But when this pride is given room to flex, it robs you of joy unless you're stepping over everyone around you. You tolerate people as long as they bolster your self-esteem. As long as you get to be in the driver's seat, everything is good. A husband like this has such a fragile ego that he demands service. A husband like this is riddled with insecurities. He doesn't know how to walk side by side with another person. He doesn't know how to let another person have the spotlight.

This brings me to another, more contemporary philosopher: Phil Jackson, the Zen master himself. My two favorite NBA basketball teams of all time are the Bulls and the Lakers. I don't really follow either team now because I've turned into a fair-weather fan for both. But my fanaticism was based on the personalities on the teams, not the logos on the jerseys. I liked Jordan and Pippen for the Bulls and Shaq and Kobe for the Lakers. The Bulls won six championships, and the Lakers won three. Many credit the success to Phil Jackson's coaching of both teams. Jackson might go down as the greatest coach of all time. He is to be credited for sure for the success, but listen to his thoughts on the subject:

> The real reason the Bulls won six NBA championships in nine years is that we plugged into the power of oneness instead of the power of one man. Sure, we had Michael Jordan, and you have to credit his talent. . . . It doesn't matter how good individual players are—they can't compete with a team that is awake and aware and trusts each other. People don't understand that. Most of the time, everybody's so concerned about not being disrespected. . . . But when we lose our fear of that, and look to each other, then vulnerability turns into strength, and we can take responsibility for our place in the larger context

> of the team and embrace a vision in which the group imperative takes precedence over personal glory.[2]

It could be argued that the reason for the success of these teams was submission. It is pretty clear that a lack of submission between Kobe and Shaq short-circuited the Lakers' championship run.

Submitting to other people is hard. Submitting to your spouse is even harder! One of the most painful verses in the Bible, which is located in a discussion about marriage, is Ephesians 5:21: "[Submit] to one another out of reverence for Christ." It is one thing to know that you are to submit; it is quite another thing to know *how* and *when* to submit. But listen to Coach Jackson on its benefits:

It is one thing to know that you are to submit; it is quite another thing to know *how* and *when* to submit.

> When a player surrenders his self-interest for the greater good, his fullest gifts as an athlete are manifested. He's not trying to force a shot, or do something that's not in his repertoire of basketball moves, or impose his personality on the team. It's funny—by playing within his natural abilities, he activates a higher potential beyond his abilities, a higher potential for the team. It changes things for everybody.[3]

THE HEART OF SUBMISSION

Just as proper submission on a team leads to victory, so submission in marriage leads to success. Marriage is not a competition or a battle to be won by one side or the other. It is a complex partnership in which both spouses are respected, loved, honored, and given space to grow and flourish. Marriage is a place where we want our spouses to win more than we want it for ourselves. It's a place where we learn to enjoy our spouses' successes as much as our own and grieve their failures with compassion and empathy.

PRINCIPLES OF SUBMISSION

YOU AND YOUR WIFE ARE EQUAL BEFORE GOD

One of the beautiful truths in the Bible is that men and women are of equal value before God. This principle was a slap in the face to the chauvinistic, patriarchal cultures in which both the Old and the New Testaments were written. Simply put, men and women have equal dignity before God.

YOU AND YOUR WIFE HAVE DIFFERING ROLES

Spouses should submit to each other's strengths. Your wife does some things better than you do. Maybe she is better at handling a crisis, planning events, or comforting a kid who has a scrape on his knee. Where she is strong, submit to her and follow. Where you are strong or have spiritual responsibility, lead.[4]

SPOUSES SHOULD SUBMIT TO EACH OTHER REGULARLY

I am a cheapskate. I inherited this from my parents. My favorite saying in this realm is that "if it's free, it's for me." Last year Amie came home with the exciting news that our oldest child needed braces. The situation grew more exciting when she told me the braces would cost five grand. I immediately activated my inner bargain hunter. I found a friend of a friend who was an orthodontist and read my blog and listened to my sermons. I called the good doctor and asked if five grand seemed excessive. To my dismay, she said no. But later, she e-mailed me and offered to pay for everything regarding our daughter's braces as a token of her gratefulness for my ministry to her. The only catch was that we had to travel forty-five minutes away for the appointments.

I declared the good news to my wife: "We are going to save five grand, and our daughter will have movie-star-quality teeth!" To my surprise, she started to cry. She explained that she had done the research and chosen an orthodontist (not the free one) based on her schedule, as well as convenience and proximity. My argument was money; hers was family. I realized that my wife is usually right when it comes to family. When I submit to her regularly in this area, we win. In this case, free was not for us. We are five grand lighter, but our family health was worth the investment.

WHEN SHOULD I SUBMIT TO MY WIFE?

There are no hard and fast rules about when this should happen, but here are some guiding principles:

1. When your wife has more expertise or life experience, or when the decision falls in an area of her strength.
2. When your wife has a strong leaning or gut feeling and you don't, even after you've intentionally thought through the situation.
3. When your wife has more invested in a potential outcome than you do, or when she will be more affected by the decision than you are.
4. When you sense that you're just trying to win or get your way more than you're trying to do what's best for you and your family.
5. When you have an opportunity to honor your wife's preferences just because you love her, and doing so will bring her joy.

I tend to be a visionary, big-picture person, while Amie is more in tune with details and logistics. I often have great ideas, but Amie helps me stay in tune with reality and the potential cost of the ideas. Because of this, I regularly submit to her about whether an idea is workable. On the other hand, because Amie greatly respects my ability to see farther ahead and from a broader perspective than she naturally does, she regularly submits to my encouragement to take risks and consider things that feel too far away or too big. Neither of us is right all the time, but we'd be foolish not to lean into each other's strengths in these areas.

Five Good Questions

1. In what areas do you wish I would submit to you?
2. In what areas do you wish I was a better leader?
3. What do you think are my strengths?
4. Where do you need specific encouragement?
5. Where are both of us weak?

CHAPTER 9

PURSUE

Most men pursue pleasure with such breathless haste that they hurry past it.

—Søren Kierkegaard

IN *THE DUDE'S GUIDE TO MANHOOD*, I CHALLENGED MEN not to let *faithfulness* become a code word for *passivity.* We can keep the letter of the law when it comes to our vows but not the spirit of them. Our wives want to know that we will stick with them through thick and thin, but they also want more than a passionless business arrangement. The only thing better than reading that chapter is getting a full chapter on the subject from Amie.[1] You'll learn from her about pursuit and why it's important. You'll hear about what happens when it's missing and practical ways to start anew.

Darrin and I met and started dating in high school. He was handsome, fun, and impressive in a million ways. He also had a lot of rough edges and growing up to do. But even then I saw something in him that made me wonder whether he might be the man I would marry someday. Several years later and shortly before Darrin popped the question, I was perplexed by some changes in his behavior. He wanted to be with me all the time. He was extremely sentimental, romantic, and protective. I loved this new side of him. It wasn't that I didn't appreciate or enjoy these behaviors, but we had dated for a long time with several on-again, off-again stretches. Honestly, I thought we were past that crazy-in-love phase. I didn't know that he had decided I was the one for him and had fallen crazy in love with me all over again.

I was over the moon when he totally surprised me with a proposal in front of our closest friends. I loved every moment of our newly engaged bliss. We had a wonderful engagement, a beautiful wedding, and a fun honeymoon. But I'd be stretching the truth if I said that Darrin continued pursuing me in the early years of our marriage as intentionally as he did when we were engaged. We were thrilled to be married, but it was hard work to learn to live with each other.

The realities of everyday life set in, and I began to experience a vague, nagging sense of disappointment at how little my husband seemed to pursue me. We were great friends and roommates, but he didn't behave as if he was completely enamored with me anymore. I knew that Darrin loved me and was committed to me, but he wasn't doing much to make that an everyday reality. I chalked it up to normal newlywed adjustment. I reminded myself that marriage isn't a fairy tale, but deep down, I couldn't rid myself of the desire to know that my husband loved and treasured me above all others.

I still wanted to be pursued.

WHAT IS PURSUIT?

A woman's desire to be rightly and intentionally pursued by a man reflects her deep longing to be known, loved, and enjoyed. The idea of pursuit conveys more than a leisurely or halfhearted endeavor. Just as images of a police pursuit or a messenger on a galloping horse display urgency and intensity, a man's pursuit of a woman is not a halfhearted or casually planned undertaking.

> A woman's desire to be rightly and intentionally pursued by a man reflects her deep longing to be known, loved, and enjoyed.

While women often settle for being pursued for sex, a woman's desire for pursuit by a man is a much more holistic and complex need. It involves being intimately known on physical, mental, emotional, and spiritual levels. We can swim around the surface of each of those areas with casual friends or acquaintances, but marriage requires continually going deep in all of them. This does not happen overnight but is cultivated over years.

A single dramatic, romantic moment makes for a compelling scene in a movie, but the real battle for a woman's heart is won by small, frequent, and strategic moves. A woman wants a man to really go after her heart over the long haul. A man needs patience as trust is built slowly and carefully. Tenacity and perseverance are necessary in this kind of pursuit that communicates security and love to a woman. Anyone can sweep in with romantic drama, but only a man of character and growing maturity can love his wife well day after day, year after year.

In short, pursuit is a personal, intentional, and specific commitment to actively love your wife where she is right now and to be intimately involved in the process of who she is becoming. Pursuit is a lifelong endeavor, not a one-time conquest, just as dating is not a race, and the wedding day is not a finish line. When a man chooses to marry a woman, he commits to a lifelong pursuit of her alone.

WHY IS PURSUIT IMPORTANT?

Pursuit is not important because a woman can't take care of herself or must have a man to meet her needs. It doesn't replace a woman's responsibility to understand who she is and what her life is about, nor is it about creating a one-sided, codependent relationship. It is not just giving your wife whatever she wants or appeasing her; rather, it is living out concern for her long-term good, whatever the cost. It is reminding her of who God has made her to be and calling out the best in her, being appropriately challenging and giving constructive criticism while serving as her most enthusiastic cheerleader and source of encouragement.

Our culture sends women mixed messages: we are to accept ourselves unconditionally as we are, yet we are to be our best in every area, doing more better and faster. Even the healthiest and most mature women struggle mightily with demands from others and themselves. When a woman feels enjoyed by her husband regularly for who she is, not for how she performs, he reinforces the truth that even when she isn't productive, successful, or perfect, she is still valuable and loved just because she is herself.

I definitely struggle with believing that my worth is determined by how much I accomplish and how useful I am to the people around me. Truthfully, my mood is much too easily influenced by my ability to cross things off my to-do list and stay on top of my schedule. I can be in a serious panic by noon if the day isn't going according to plan. I've come a long way in the process of believing that I'm not what I do and living from that belief, but I've by no means arrived.

Because Darrin knows me better and more intimately than anyone else does, he is tremendously influential in helping me believe and live from this truth. He understands how destructive it is to my soul to live as if my primary purpose is to be productive and useful. He appreciates all the ways that I'm capable and competent, yet he reminds me that those things are not really who I am, nor do they define why I'm valuable to him or to God. He asks questions when he sees me slipping into familiar but harmful patterns and patiently dialogues with me about my responses. I'm stubborn and don't always respond well to blatant confrontation, even if I know it's right. But hearing him ask, "You seem really frantic right now. Why is that?" or "Why do you feel that you need to get all of this done today?" opens the door for me to examine my heart and actions and talk about them.

WHAT HAPPENS WHEN A WIFE IS REGULARLY PURSUED BY HER HUSBAND?

Having Darrin intentionally and regularly pursue me dramatically changes the trajectory of our marriage. Little things make a big difference. Once, on a challenging road trip with our kids, when at least one child had already gotten carsick and thrown up in the car, Darrin walked out of a gas station with a bag of my favorite candy, which doesn't happen to be his favorite candy. We were tired, stressed, and ready to be home, but Darrin had taken a moment to consider what I would enjoy in that moment. That little gesture spoke volumes to me without his saying a word. It was like setting a reset button and reminded me that we were on the same team. Darrin made it easier to look ahead to the day when this road trip would be a funny story that we'd tell together, as opposed to just being miserable in the moment.

Trusting Darrin is easier for me when I see his commitment to my good in practical ways. When he takes a genuine interest in my desires and preferences, even in something small such as the music played in the car or the pillow fluffed up for me to sleep on, I feel honored, enjoyed, and appreciated.

Over time, I'm more open to Darrin's constructive criticism and less defensive as I more deeply understand and believe that I am valued and important to him. I become more comfortable asking for help and input when Darrin asks me what I need and how he can help, instead of choosing to do it his way or thinking mostly about what would benefit him.

WHAT HAPPENS WHEN A WIFE ISN'T PURSUED?

When women aren't intentionally and consistently pursued by their husbands, they tend to look for something to fill that void.

In the years shortly after we planted the church, Darrin struggled to pursue me well. He was working an insane number of hours and felt tremendous pressure to succeed. He was distracted by endless demands and struggled with setting healthy boundaries related to his time and energy. Although I empathized with his stress and was extremely proud of his hard work and commitment, I was really lonely. I see this mostly in retrospect because I kept very busy with our young children, our home, and my ministry work during this time. After a while, I had to admit that I felt more like a business partner than a wife. I sadly told Darrin that no one else was pursuing me, but it would be tempting to enjoy the attention if someone was.

Unfortunately, over the years in ministry, we've seen a lot of wives who are struggling with inattentiveness and a lack of pursuit from their husbands. It's usually not the first thing that a wife will flat-out admit because admitting that she doesn't feel desired and pursued by her husband is an incredibly vulnerable statement. But that woundedness tends to come out in one way or another. When women aren't intentionally and consistently pursued by their husbands, they tend to look for something to fill that void.

Romantic movies or books allow for an escape from reality that appears to fill that need for a short time. These escapes actually end up leading to deeper disappointment when reality sets in or when a husband's real-life attempts at pursuit fall dramatically short of the scripted on-screen comparison. I've definitely been enamored with a character's romantic behavior in a book or movie and then been really annoyed and discontented with Darrin shortly thereafter. That's probably not a coincidence!

Many women quit waiting for men to pursue them in dating relationships and decide to become the pursuers. There's nothing wrong with a woman putting herself in situations where she's more likely to meet new people with similar interests or values, or even letting her friends know that she's interested in a dating relationship. And it's important for a married woman to also pursue her husband for the purpose of loving and serving him well. There are countless areas of life where it is wise for women to initiate and take the lead. But aggressively pursuing men for the purpose of dating can send a mixed message.

How can a woman know whether a man will have the courage and perseverance to know and love her well over the course of a lifetime if she doesn't expect that from the beginning? A man may feel that he is experiencing a bait and switch when a woman starts out by taking most or all of the initiative in a relationship and then turns the tables and asks him to take on that role.

When I look back on our dating relationship, I wish I had a different expectation regarding Darrin's pursuit of me because it set an unhealthy precedent for our marriage that we've had to work hard to overcome. Granted, we started dating when we were very young, and we probably had no business dating at that time at all. Yet I regret not holding him to higher standards. I was always available and low maintenance, and I rarely asked for my preferences to be honored. These behaviors probably came from a fear of losing the relationship, and decisions made out of fear are rarely good ones. It's always wise to start the way that you want to end up; and in this case, it would have been better to expect Darrin to diligently pursue my heart from the beginning and to accept nothing less.

WHEN SHE'S NOT PURSUED

A woman tends to respond to a lack of pursuit by doing the following:

- Withdrawing (out of fear of continuing to be disappointed)
- Being passive-aggressive or exhibiting attention-seeking behavior
- Feeling bitterness and anger

- Doubting the character of her husband and the security of her marriage
- Questioning her worth and value as a person and a woman

WHAT DOES PURSUIT LOOK LIKE IN MARRIAGE?

INITIATING

I greatly appreciate when Darrin takes initiative in our marriage. He's definitely a take-charge kind of guy at work and in other areas, but initiating in marriage is less of a personality thing and more of an everyday decision. It's not a task to cross off the list. Initiating in marriage means taking intentional steps to let your wife know that she is treasured and valued.

Initiating doesn't look the same in every marriage. It generally involves not just waiting around for your wife to do something but taking responsibility for it yourself. You don't have to be in the lead in every single situation. Rather, you are willing and looking for opportunities to do so with a heart to serve. If you don't know where to start, ask your wife where she would like you to take more initiative in your marriage.

Here are some places to start:

- Ask your wife's opinion on something and follow up with clarifying questions.
- Look for opportunities for fun dates, family events, or vacations.

- Take responsibility for planning details for date nights or time together as a couple.

PRIORITIZING

Prioritizing means that how you spend your time and energy reflects your wife's importance to you. Merely declaring that she's a priority doesn't mean much, especially if she doesn't feel she is. If you really want to know how you're doing in this area, ask her. She's the expert. If she feels that she's a high priority, she probably is. If she doesn't, she's probably not.

One of the biggest fights that Darrin and I ever had was about his travel schedule. I didn't feel that I was a high priority. Darrin didn't feel that I understood the stressful complexity of his job and the responsibilities he was juggling. We went round and round, arguing the same points and missing each other every time. Finally, I started crying and yelled, "I want to actually get to be with you! I picked you because I like you more than anybody else, and I want to be with you more than other people get to be with you. And I want to know that you feel that way about me too."

> Priorities are always about who has our hearts, and in marriage, we want to know that our hearts belong to each other.

Well, that finally got us to the heart of the matter that we'd been missing. I wanted to feel that I was his priority, and Darrin wanted to know that he was mine. He had just gotten a little lost in thinking that I should demonstrate that by accommodating all the chaos in his life. Embarrassed, sad, and humbled, he replied, "That's probably the nicest thing that anyone's ever said to me."

Prioritizing sounds as if it's about calendars, time management, and choices, and to some degree, that's true. But priorities are always about who has our hearts, and in marriage, we want to know that our hearts belong to each other.

KEEP CHIVALRY ALIVE

Most women appreciate men with good manners who demonstrate chivalrous behaviors. This falls into the category of pursuit because it demonstrates respect and honor for your wife. This is not about her being unable to open a door or pull out a chair for herself; it is a practical way for you to demonstrate humble everyday care and pursuit. It's easy to become sloppy with these things when we're incredibly comfortable with another person, but comfort shouldn't be equated with complacency and disinterest.

Here are practical examples:

- Open doors for your wife, including the car door.
- Let her enter a room first.
- Pull out a chair for her at a restaurant.
- Use good table manners.
- Include words like *please* and *thank you* in your vocabulary with her. If you wouldn't want someone else to take her for granted or use less-than-respectful words, treat her with that same kindness.

PURSUE YOUR WIFE PHYSICALLY

Our physical bodies are incredibly important because they're the vehicles through which we experience everything in this life, including many aspects of marriage.

Being physically affectionate in nonsexual ways

Sex is a big part of physical pursuit, but it is only one aspect of it. Having physical contact and expressing affection in ways that aren't necessarily sexual build intimate connection and closeness into our everyday lives. If you come from a home where this was not the norm, doing this may feel unnatural or uncomfortable at first, but give it a little time. Look for a few practical ways to incorporate physical touch into your everyday life together:

- Start and end the day with some kind of physical touch.
- Sit close to her and hold her hand when you're watching TV or a movie.
- Embrace your wife when she's upset or crying.
- Do something physical together. For example, exercise, take walks, or do yard work.
- Show active concern for her physical health and needs. Help her work out logistics for regular exercise, sleep, and balanced meals.

    Body image is a challenging issue for many women. Be aware of and sensitive to any struggle that your wife may have in this area. Become a primary source of encouragement for her.

- Take responsibility for your physical health.

  Your wife benefits when you feel better, have more energy, and live a long and healthy life. With the right focus, doing this is one of the kindest and most romantic things you can do for your wife. It's not about you; it's about her.

Sex

Many men think that they know a lot about sex, but the goal is to know about what pleases your wife sexually and what works for you as a couple to create a healthy and fun sex life in your marriage.[2] *Do your homework, honor your wife's preferences, and be sensitive to her sexual history. Many women have suffered sexual abuse and/or violence and have experienced emotional trauma and confusion because of it. Other women have significant guilt and shame with regard to previous consensual sexual relationships before marriage. Healing from past wounds takes time and patience, and professional help from an experienced and compassionate counselor is often necessary. Part of pursuing your wife physically is learning how to pursue her sexually in ways that feel romantic, enjoyable, and exciting for her, not just for you.*

Part of pursuing your wife physically is learning how to pursue her sexually in ways that feel romantic, enjoyable, and exciting for her, not just for you.

PURSUE YOUR WIFE MENTALLY

- Initiate conversations with your wife on topics that are interesting to both of you, such as music, books, current events, or sports. Let her teach you about something that is interesting to her. Ask questions that will help you understand the topic better. Read something or listen to something together, and talk about it.

  My background is in music, and Darrin regularly asks me specific questions about a song on the radio, a particular artist, or genre. He respects my knowledge and experience in this area and demonstrates that by the questions he asks me. We both love baseball, but Darrin is much more knowledgeable than I am about it. I regularly ask him questions when we watch games together, and I enjoy the game even more as I learn more about it.
- Talk to her about her job: what she loves, what challenges her, and what she's currently working on. This is equally important for a stay-at-home mom. Asking, "What did you do all day?" is not the right question.
- Engage your wife in conversation about your children—their development, goals for them, education, and concerns. Darrin and I talk a lot

about the funny or interesting things that our kids do and say.

- Surprise your wife with an opportunity to pursue something that is mentally interesting or challenging to her, such as a class, a retreat, or a weekend trip. Look for articles, books, or resources that will be interesting to her, and initiate conversation about them.

PURSUE YOUR WIFE EMOTIONALLY

When I don't feel connected to Darrin, the first place I notice it is on an emotional level. We may be on the same page about the many details and logistics that we manage on an everyday basis, but if it's been awhile since we've laughed together or honestly shared our worries and concerns, it's hard to feel that I know Darrin or am known by him. We've worked hard to keep a weekly date in our schedule for many years, but a few years ago, we added a weekly planning meeting. We realized that our dates could easily be dominated by all the logistical and practical things that we legitimately need to talk about, but those conversations did little to help us build emotional intimacy in our marriage.

Darrin struggles the most in pursuing me in this area. As he becomes a healthier and more emotionally engaged man, it's easier for him to pursue me in this way. If he chooses instead to be emotionally shut down, he turns into fix-it guy and treats me as a problem to be solved with a few simple steps. The reality is that I'm more emotionally mature than Darrin, and he needs me to help him grow on this level. I've had to learn that one of the best gifts I can offer Darrin is the strength and resolve not to settle for an emotionally disconnected husband.

He's had to take risks in expressing his heart to me and pursuing my heart in ways that don't come naturally to him. When Darrin talks about areas where he's struggling, failing, or feeling vulnerable, I think more highly of him, not less. I feel loved and appreciated when he works at being romantic, even if his efforts don't result in a perfect moment. There's something, too, about emotional connectedness and trust that seem to spill over into all other areas of marriage. We just generally enjoy each other more when our hearts are aligned. We have more fun together, our sexual relationship improves, and we are less pulled apart by the grind of everyday life.

Here are some suggestions:

- Do the work of becoming an emotionally healthy person so that you can process your emotions with your wife. Think through how you feel about particular situations or events and talk to her about your feelings. You can't lead your wife somewhere you're not willing to go.
- Accept that your wife may experience and process emotions very differently from the way that you do. Give her space to do that without judgment or impatience.
- Learn to ask questions that draw your wife out emotionally:

    - "How do you feel about that?"
    - "Why does that makes you sad, angry, or happy?"
    - "What do you wish had happened instead?"
- Give her room to experience and process her emotions without immediately offering solutions or a different perspective. If she doesn't specifically ask for either of those things, it's likely that she just wants to be understood.
- Do more listening than talking in emotional conversations.
- Know whether your wife is primarily an internal processor (works things out by thinking about them) or an external processor (works things out by talking about them), and honor her wiring in that. Internal processors need space for silence and thinking and freedom to revisit a topic after thinking about it more thoroughly. External processors need to be able to work things out verbally without their listeners making immediate judgments.
- Have conversations with your wife about the emotional climate of the home in which she grew up and how that has affected the way she processes emotions today, and vice versa.
- Learn about the different stages of grief, postpartum depression, or other life circumstances that affect your wife's emotional health. Seek a

professional counselor when you hit a roadblock. Seeking professional counseling help doesn't mean that your marriage is a total disaster. It just means that you need a little help, which is completely normal and to be expected. Every married couple should probably seek professional help at some point in their marriage.

- Learn to create healthy boundaries in your life with emotionally unhealthy people, and help your wife to do the same thing. Members of your extended family are definitely included in this category.

Every married couple should probably seek professional help at some point in their marriage.

PURSUE YOUR WIFE SPIRITUALLY

This is the deepest and most important way that a husband pursues his wife. Nothing makes me feel more pursued and cared about than when Darrin shows concern and interest for my spiritual well-being.

- Take responsibility for the spiritual climate in your home and the spiritual growth of your family.
- Research churches in the area where you live, and lead the process of finding a good fit for your family. Be involved in church. Help your wife get

the family ready for church services. Doing this can be really stressful, particularly when your children are young.

- Ask your wife questions about her relationship with God. Talk to her about what God is doing in your life and what you are learning about yourself.
- Give your wife space and time to notice changes in you that are a result of spiritual growth instead of trying to convince her that you're changing and growing. Actions over the long haul speak louder than words. Sometimes a wife needs a little time to believe that a change is real and will last.
- Pray for your wife regularly.
- Encourage your wife to pursue friendships and opportunities that are spiritually challenging and inspiring.

If you've been humbled by the reality that you've done a poor job pursuing your wife, it's not too late to take action and turn the ship around. Don't waste any time before telling her that you know you've failed in pursuing her heart, and offer a sincere and thought-out apology. Follow up quickly with specific and intentional action, as well as long-term plans for how you're going to continue pursuing your wife on an ongoing basis. Find some men who do this well and are willing to help you be accountable to follow through with your intentions. Ask your wife regularly how you're doing and how you can improve. And never give up. Your wife is a treasure, and your marriage is worth it.

Five Good Questions

1. How did I pursue you when we were dating?
2. In what area (physical, mental, emotional, or spiritual) do I pursue you the most? The least?
3. How do you think our marriage is negatively affected when I don't pursue you well?
4. What feels romantic to you?
5. Do you feel pursued by me?

CHAPTER 10

WORSHIP

Thou hast made us for thyself, O Lord, and our heart is restless until it finds its rest in thee.

—Augustine

ALL I COULD THINK ABOUT WHEN I WAS A KID WAS sports. Summers were heaven for me, getting up in the morning with nothing to do but play. I organized my life around connecting with my friends. We played basketball, football, and Wiffle ball almost every day. When my friends weren't around, I played by myself. I took a worn-out tennis ball and threw it against the side of our red brick ranch house. I played through lunch, rarely eating anything during the day. When my mom called me in for supper, I scarfed down whatever was on the plate and hightailed it back to play whatever sport was on the docket that night. I played until we couldn't see the ball anymore, and I came in and went to sleep, dreaming about playing professional sports. I got up the next day, rinsed, and repeated step one.

My approach to sports was my dad's approach to work. Armed with only a tenth-grade education, my dad did quite well for himself. He was an excavator by day and an entrepreneur by night. He single-handedly turned eighty uncultivated acres into a premier subdivision with thirty houses. He cleared all the trees, rerouted all the creeks, and buttressed the dam, which enabled a five-acre lake to thrive. He built the infrastructure of roads and sewers as well as the first few houses. He literally worked eighteen hours a day and then collapsed for a few hours. He woke up and went to his day job, where he daydreamed about how to make the subdivision even better.

What was going on with father and son? Well, I was a kid. Kids play. Athletic kids play sports. Kids do (or used to) play outside all day. I was not a unique snowflake. Neither was my dad. Plenty of men work two jobs or tons of hours. What is unusual is not that I played and Dad worked. What was a little unusual was how play and work consumed every waking hour and even our subconscious. I remember talking to Dad about this dynamic when I was in college. He said, "Darrin, I eat work, sleep work, and dream work."

Human beings are predictable this way. Some of us are passionate in our devotion to work or play or family. Others of us are milder in our pursuits. But every human being must put something other than him- or herself at the center.

We have this need to give ourselves to something larger than ourselves. That need is worship.

When I was first exploring spirituality, some Christians told me to read the Bible. Doing that was a challenge because all I had read until that point were a few force-fed classics by well-meaning high school teachers and *Sports Illustrated*. Now I was reading this voluminous ancient text and trying to make sense of it.

I was always afraid of the Bible. To me that big black book with the superthin pages represented thousands of rules I never could keep. That kept me from reading it. What I didn't know couldn't hurt me. Maybe God would let me plead ignorance.

The first story was about a couple who broke the rules and were banished from Paradise. That was my first reading of this story. Largely because I wasn't fond of authority, I thought the story went something like this: God created a garden. He put a man and a woman in it. He arbitrarily told them not to eat the fruit, but they did, so he kicked them out.

But as I studied, I began to see a deeper story. Adam and Eve were created to worship. God had created mountains and moons, stars and seas to display the glory of the Creator. Adam and Eve were to do the same as God's prized creation. They were like mirrors that reflected some aspects of God. The idea seems to be that our first parents and their children were intended to be reminders on the earth that God was present, good, and loving.[1]

The first humans were created to have God at the center of their beings. They initially saw life as a gift from God, and they returned the gift to the Giver in worship. But as I kept reading and learning, I realized that worship isn't just vertical to God; it is horizontal for the world. Adam and Eve were given a mandate: "Be fruitful and multiply and fill the earth and subdue it, and have dominion over the fish of the sea and over the birds of the heavens and over every living thing that moves on the earth" (Gen. 1:28). They were called to worship God by ruling over God's creation in God's name. That is, as they went out into the world as a couple, they were on a mission together.

Being made in the image of God means that we are to represent God. Anthony Hoekema wrote,

> Man, then, was created in God's image so that he or she might represent God, like an ambassador from a foreign country. As an ambassador represents his country's authority, so man (both male and female) must represent the authority of God. As an ambassador is concerned to advance the best interests of his country, so man must seek to advance God's program for this world. As God's representatives, we should support and defend what God stands for, and should promote what God promotes. As God's representatives, we must not do what we like, but what God desires. Through us God works out his purposes on this earth.[2]

Adam and Eve believed the lie that we all believe: they could become their own God, be the arbiters of their own truth, and live the life that God had given them in their own strength. We have followed the paths of our first parents, apart from the short stint in Paradise they enjoyed. Our mission is out of focus, and God's image has been marred and broken. This brokenness that we experience doesn't prevent us from having decent marriages or doing good things in the world. But we have lost something that affects everything in us and around us because we have misplaced worship.

> Human beings are made to worship. The easiest thing to worship is ourselves.

Human beings are made to worship. The easiest thing to worship is ourselves. This worship is even trinitarian in nature: me, myself, and I. It sounds weird to say that we worship ourselves. I mean, do any of us really believe that we are God? No. But as my friend said in a moment of honesty, "I know that I am not *the* God, yet I act like I am *a* god." We all act this way. But how?

WE DO THINGS FOR OUR OWN GLORY

One of the more interesting concepts I have learned in the realm of theology in recent years is the God-centeredness of God.[3] Part of what this means is that God is the only being in the universe who can be selfish and be justified in doing so. God is about being glorified because he is worthy. It is right and just for God to desire to be adored and worshiped. And when God receives his rightful glory, the world receives its desired joy.[4] Worshiping God gives God his due as the most glorious being in the world, and it grants us peace and joy as we do what we were made to do.

When our worship is misplaced, we do things not for God's glory but for our own. A reality of human brokenness is that our sight is mostly fixed upon ourselves. Even when we do good things for others, it is really about us. Take this parable for instance:

> There once was a king of grace and wealth. One day, he noticed that the land next to his kingdom had great carrots growing there. He found the farmer who was responsible and complimented him on his field and produce. The next day, the farmer came and presented himself before the king, saying, "O good king, you have acted justly and ruled wisely. I want to present you this carrot. The best one I've ever grown, perhaps the best I will ever grow. It's my pride. I want you to have it as a token of my appreciation for all the good things that you have done for our land." The king, overjoyed by this gift, said in front of all his noblemen to the farmer, "I own the fields surrounding yours. I'd like you to have an acre so that you can continue to grow these wonderful crops for our people."
>
> The next day one of the noblemen came and presented himself before the king, saying, "O good king, you have ruled wisely and justly. The kingdom and our land are more safe and secure than they have ever been. I

raise horses and would love for you to have this—my best horse—as a token of my appreciation for all the good that you have done." The king received the horse, thanking the nobleman. The nobleman looked at the king, waiting for him to continue speaking. When he realized it wasn't going to happen, he began to walk off.

The king spoke up, discerning his heart, "Now, wait a moment. You overheard what I did for the farmer yesterday, didn't you? The farmer gave me a carrot and you gave me this horse, but that's not the only difference. The farmer was giving me the carrot, but you were giving yourself the horse."[5]

WE BELIEVE OUR VIEW IS GOD'S VIEW

We live in an age of tolerance. Most people would say that others' views should be respected no matter what. This works until the supermajority of people have a certain take about a moral issue. Then the mob rules. We may act as if we are tolerant, but most of us secretly wish that others would just get on board with the truth (our take).

WE EXPECT OTHERS TO TREAT US LIKE GOD

There is nothing more enraging than when people don't give us our due—whether it is credit at work or praise at home. Something deep within us wants to be honored, respected, and adored. Every human desires to gain other humans' praise and, dare I say, worship. The problem shows up in our emotional lives when we expect others to treat us like God. We rarely state this expectation out loud, but it expresses itself through common, problematic emotions. Envy says, "Life owes me." Guilt says, "I owe you." Greed says, "I owe me." And anger says, "You (people or God) owe me." This expectation turns our marriages into debt-debtor relationships.

WHEN THE GODS HIDE

We do worship ourselves, but we also worship *with ourselves.* That is, we expend our time, our talent, and our treasure somewhere. Self-worship gets boring. At some point all of us look to something other than ourselves to focus on. We feel an interior compulsion to rest our lives upon *something or someone* outside ourselves. The human spirit demands an object on which to set its hope. We simply must go to someone or something to feel at peace. We have to express our worship to something or someone.

As I kept reading the Bible, I came across this character called Moses. Moses was filled with ambition. He grew up in a palace, though he was really a slave. God called him to lead his people from slavery, but he got ahead of the call and killed a slaveholder in order to jump-start his mission from God. As a murderer, Moses had to run for his life into the wilderness where he spent forty years tending sheep before God used him to lead Israel from slavery to the promised land.

Moses was the guy to whom God entrusted the Ten Commandments. He went up to a mountain with his hands empty and came back with ten laws: don't murder, don't lie, don't cheat on your wife, don't hate on Mom and Dad, stuff like that. This made sense to me. As I read these laws from God, I thought, *Keep these rules, and God will accept me.* Then I tried keeping the Ten Commandments. It didn't go well. I failed early and often. I, like many of you, was honestly seeking God. Did God want me to feel like a failure? Was spirituality in general and Christianity in specific about failing to keep rules and then feeling guilty for breaking them?

The first two commandments that God gave Moses didn't address horizontal sins (against other human beings) such as cheating, lying, and stealing; misplaced worship was their focus. God gave us ten commandments, only ten! These two seemed to set the tone for the rest of the commandments.[6] As I read the Old Testament, I kept seeing this word *idolatry*, which is the Bible's word for misplaced worship. God sent prophets to warn his people about misplaced worship. The prophets condemned them for putting so much of their energy, passion, and time into little gods that were not worthy of such attention. They pleaded for them not to waste their one and only life serving a god that was not worthy, worshiping something that would eventually fail them.

Scripture teaches us that human beings ultimately will look either to the one, true God or to some other god. Our functional gods take various forms—persons, places, or things. We gain our identity and give our worship to God or something else—success, relationships, possessions, family, or reputation.

We simply must worship something. Whatever gets our worship gets our lives. Our word *worship* is from the Old English *weorthscipe* ("worth shape"). Whatever we deem most worthy shapes everything—our behaviors, motivations, daydreams, and actions.[7]

This is why the Bible doesn't treat idolatry as a sin, as it does gluttony, lust, or lying. It treats idolatry as *the only alternative to worshiping and loving the one true God*.[8] Sin happens because we treasure our idols more than we love our God. When we don't actively love God, we actively love something else. When God is not the center of our lives, something else will step in.

The first married couple were on a mission to worship God and subdue the world together. They held strong views as God's image bearers but didn't hold them above God's word. They were able to serve and love each other without gaining their identities from their service and love. They were able to be served and loved by each other without demanding to be worshiped.

> When God is not the center of our lives, something else will step in.

You may be asking a very important question: "What does this have to do with marriage?" Simply put, everything. Let me explain. The clearest teaching in the Bible on marriage is found in the New Testament book of Ephesians. It gives us a strange metaphor for marriage that even the human author of this ancient text called a mystery (Eph. 5:25–32). The apostle Paul, who was the human author of Ephesians, said that a relationship between a man and a woman in marriage is like the relationship between Jesus Christ and his church. The text makes several points:

- Jesus is the groom who pursues the bride (his people).
- Jesus sacrifices his life for his bride.
- Jesus leads in forgiveness for his bride.
- Jesus is committed to bring out the beauty of his bride.

Husbands, this is your charge. This whole book has been one big challenge for you to be for your wife as Christ is for the church. If we want our marriages to flourish, we need to become husbands who can listen to the hearts of our wives and engage them in conversation about our own. We are called to appropriately confront our wives and humbly be confronted by our wives. As we model healthy rhythms of work and rest, we are to continually grow intellectually, socially, and emotionally. We are called to lead our wives spiritually and serve them sacrificially.

But there is a problem: we can't do this. If I can do one of those things well in a given day, I'm thrilled. Some of us are trying, but if we are honest, we are failing. We will fail to be perfect and fail to be what our wives want. We can make our effort an idol and keep trying harder to please our brides. We can keep reading marriage books and set out to be perfect husbands. But we will fail because the effort god is not strong enough to help us be the husbands we are called to be. We can make our wives idols and direct our worship, adoration, focus, and attention to them. The problem is that they will fail us. Being God is a weight that is too great to bear, even for our wonderful wives.

Idolatry will kill us. Our god-substitutes leave us empty and powerless to be the men we were created to be. Our wives do not want our ultimate worship; they want husbands who know where their ultimate worship should go. They want men who know God, are led by God, and love like God loves. This is possible because of Jesus.

Our wives do not want our ultimate worship; they want husbands who know where their ultimate worship should go.

Jesus is the Savior who will not fail you. While he was on the earth, he lived a perfect life devoid of misplaced worship. He was sinless, which qualified him to be our substitute. As our substitute, Jesus died on a cross to bear God's anger against our sin. Jesus was judged in our place for our sin. Three days after death, Jesus conquered death by rising from the grave.

He is God; we are not. He is the one who listens to our prayers. He is the one who always says the right words. He is the one who confronts us so that we can grow. He is the one who has worked hard so that we can rest in him. He submitted to his Father in our service. He pursued us when we weren't pursuing him. He is the only one worthy of our worship.

He is the only husband who is perfect.

This is good news for people everywhere, even imperfect husbands.

When we worship God through the person of Jesus Christ, we can experience marriage as it was intended. And here are the results of living within God's design for marriage, according to Ephesians 5:

- Submission without domination (v. 21)
- Love without manipulation (vv. 22–25)
- Sanctification without impatience (vv. 26–29)
- Oneness without codependence (v. 31)
- Separation without abandonment (v. 31)
- Happiness without isolation (vv. 30, 32)

If all this makes sense to you, pray with these words: "God, I see that I am so sinful that I can never save myself. I accept the gift of your Son, who lived perfectly so I don't have to be perfect, died brutally so I don't have to be punished, and rose from death so I don't have to live in my own strength."

If you prayed this prayer authentically, your sins are totally blotted out, and the righteousness of God is applied to you because of Christ! Also, the Holy Spirit—the third person of the Trinity—is now living in you to empower you to become more and more free of sin and more like Jesus in your character.

A great marriage takes a village. As great as your friends and family are, they will not provide the diversity that you need to excel in your marriage. You and your wife need to be around people who share your faith in Christ and desire to have excellent marriages. Both values can be actualized only in a local church.

You may come from a home that didn't equip you well to face the challenges of marriage. Your parents may be divorced. You're hoping for something deeper and more permanent. Perhaps like me, your dad didn't equip you to be the husband you desire to be. If so, there is good news. A community that helps clueless husbands like us is the church. Part of its mission is to help you have the best marriage possible.

You may be experiencing conflict and strain in your marriage right now because you're so fixated on yourself. Church gets much more interesting when you serve. So does your marriage. When you cultivate and not just consume, you'll find a renewed intimacy in a shared mission. Remember, marriage started off as a mission with a husband and a wife imaging God for a better world. My prayer is that you embrace this mission.

I can still see the befuddled look on my father's face when I asked him a couple of decades ago if he had any advice on marriage. "I'm not too good at the romance stuff," he said. I feel just like my dad on many days. But when I apply the skills that we have discussed here to marriage, I make progress. Progress is not perfection. But it is really good to know that the journey to a great marriage can be empowered by the One who was perfect.

ACKNOWLEDGMENTS

WE WOULD LIKE TO THANK AMIE'S PARENTS, CHARLIE and Marilyn McKenzie, for their unwavering support of our marriage, family, and ministry. We love you and so appreciate the example of your forty-seven-year-long marriage.

Our marriage is stronger, more joyful, and more intimate because of the amazing insight and counseling of Doug Samsel. Thank you for loving us well and helping us more deeply understand Jesus, ourselves, and one another.

We could not have written this book without the tremendous help we received from Stephen Hess, our research assistant. Thank you for keeping us on track, enforcing deadlines, and making sense of our chaos.

Stephen Deere provided profoundly helpful insight in the editing process. Thank you for pushing us to dig deeper in order to tell our story more authentically.

Darrin's assistant, Jeremy Burrows, tirelessly handles a million details with incredible thoroughness and calmness. We can't thank you enough for all the ways that you serve us and your tenacity in problem-solving.

The Journey Elder and Executive Leadership teams, and the Acts 29 Board, along with their wives, have been an amazing source of support and community. We are so honored and humbled to serve alongside you and are deeply grateful for your friendship and care.

We would also like to thank all the couples that are a little or a lot ahead of us in their marriages who have spoken truth and wisdom into our lives and let us learn from their example. Rick and Jetta McGinniss, Terry and Vicki Mohr, Lynn and Jamie Beckemeier, and Tom and Debbie Holley—our marriage is better today because of you and your willingness to be honest and challenging. Thank you.

Finally, we're so grateful to the multitude of married couples who have let us be a part of their pre- and post-marital counseling. It has been our joy and privilege to walk alongside you in learning to love well and to honor God in our marriages. Thank you for your teachable hearts and vulnerability.

APPENDIX A

WHAT IF I'M SINGLE?

I PASTOR A CHURCH THAT MINISTERS TO THOUSANDS OF singles. Over the years I have had several conversations with them about what it is like to be single in our world. Overwhelmingly, the singles report that they just don't have enough modeling or information about how to navigate in a world of couples. Here are some thoughts on how not to just survive singleness but to thrive as a single person:

ACKNOWLEDGE YOUR DISAPPOINTMENT

Not every single is disappointed with his or her life, but many are. You are disappointed with the fact that you are single. You are tired of being lonely. You are sick of your friends who are gaga over their significant others or their spouses. A lot of singles are in denial regarding their disappointment. They cover it up with their careers, routines, or constant busy-ness. Owning your disappointment takes courage. Talking to a few trusted friends or a pastor is a great place to start. It might also be wise to invest in a counseling relationship with a professional. I have a single friend who is in his forties now. He has told me repeatedly that his counselor has kept him sane through a couple of decades of unwanted singleness.

ENLARGE YOUR RELATIONAL NETWORK

Celeste was so tired of the same people. The same people at work, the same people at parties, and the same people in her apartment complex. She began to realize that although she loved her friends and many of her coworkers, they were holding her back. Friends are like mirrors in a way. They reflect an image of ourselves to us. She was sick of staring at the same mirrors, so she decided to get new ones. She joined a spinning class and met some people at the gym. She volunteered as a tutor at an elementary school and met some more. She didn't drop all her relationships, but she did prioritize new ones. Celeste is now engaged to a man she met while volunteering. He was a teacher at the school.

BUILD YOUR CAREER

You might respond to this suggestion with, "Duh!" But many singles don't invest themselves fully in their jobs. They are coasting. Either they lack ambition, or they misplace it. Singles who lack ambition confuse complacency with contentment. They've settled into a role that's not particularly challenging. They're not being asked to maximize their potential and acquire new skills. And some like it that way because they've redirected their energy and creativity into their hobbies. They don't believe it's possible for their passion and profession to align.

Some struggle to rightly view ambition because they know many driven people who have used and neglected others on the way to the top of the corporate ladder. Your father may have been one of these men. It's left you with a strong distaste for and a deficient view of work. Others (especially Millennials) have strong desires and intentions, but they don't have the discipline and persistence to grow through their current less-than-perfect jobs. Maybe you were told you could be anything you wanted to be if you had a college education. Now, reality is setting in, and it hurts. The path toward finding a satisfying job is often long and arduous.

As I wrote at length in *The Dude's Guide to Manhood*, men have been innately wired to find purpose and significance in their work. It may be suppressed or misdirected, but that call to make something of the world is still there. And I've found through years of pastoral counseling that a man's struggles in his work will carry over into his marriage. The discipline and character required to pursue one's career aspirations are also needed to pursue a woman. You won't aimlessly arrive in a satisfying job or a relationship.

BECOME MORE INTERESTING

One reality of life is that the longer we live, the more boring we become. Some of us love who we are and what we are into. We really don't care to try new things. The attitude is, "If someone can't accept me for who I am, then so what!" There is a lot of truth to this statement. I am certainly not suggesting that you deny your passions and repent of your personality. I am suggesting, however, that you get out of your comfort zone.

As I said in *The Dude's Guide to Manhood*:

> Your season as a single man is an excellent opportunity to learn about the world and find your place within it. It's a chance to acquire the sort of skills and interests that will hold people's attention when they're fifty as easily as they do when they're five. . . . So gain some skills. Learn to cook rather than simply eating out. Develop a love of reading. Learn a foreign language or two. Take up a musical instrument, and not simply because you have visions of rock stardom but because playing music is fun. Try a new sport. Stop being so boring.

ADDRESS AWKWARDNESS

Some of the most awkward people in the world are married. And some are single. What is awkward to you may not be to me and vice versa. But people can pick up some habits that might not exactly endear them to potential spouses. Your awkwardness may come from one or more of the following: personality, interests, upbringing, or narcissism.

There are other ways to be awkward. These are some

of the ways that tend to hinder interpersonal connection and relationships. For more information, visit http://www.succeedsocially.com/relatedfactors.

HANG WITH HEALTHY FAMILIES

I made several unwise decisions as a single, but one wise decision was to pick a couple of families and spend time with them. One couple was married just a couple of years and had an infant. I learned a ton by watching how the baby changed the ways this couple related to each other. I knew the couple before the baby, and it was instructive to watch them readjust expectations and learn to serve each other when their marriage was joyfully disrupted by a new life.

Another family had three children, ranging in age from five to twelve. During the time I was hanging at their house, they were going through financial difficulty. To watch this family stretch their money and set their kids' expectations about wants versus needs was amazing. I have kids these ages now, and I use the lessons I learned when I was a twenty-something single.

I also babysat for both families. Because I had time and worked for food, I was able to serve these families and learn to be responsible for someone other than myself. Singles, don't give in to the temptation to just hang with other singles. Make thoughtful choices with your free time, and your life will be more satisfying.

FOCUS YOUR FREE TIME

You will never have as much discretionary time as you do now. This is one of your grand resources in this season of life. Despite the countless opportunities in front of us, most of us are creatures of habit. When we have a free moment, we default to surfing the Internet or watching Netflix. I met with one young man who spent an entire weekend watching the *Band of Brothers* series in his apartment alone. We can quickly lose ourselves in a virtual world. And yet we wonder where all our time went. Take charge of your free time, and do something that isn't just about distracting yourself from your life.

PURSUE PURITY

Avoiding sexual sin involves dealing directly with God. Over years of counseling singles, I've noticed that though there is a physiological component to lust, the root of sexual sin is not always lust. Sometimes, it is a way of expressing one's anger or lack of control. For many, the root of sexual sin is loneliness. Turning to images on the screen becomes a means of expressing discontent with God for not providing a spouse. As you seek to set up healthy boundaries to keep you from temptation, know that you need to deal with the underlying heart issues that feed into lust. One thing I learned from being promiscuous before starting to date and eventually marry my wife was that sex outside marriage in no way prepares you for sex inside marriage. The lust we act upon with another person or ourselves breaks us apart, warring against God's plan for us to be wholly united to our spouses.

APPENDIX B

WHAT IF I'M SCARED OF COUNSELING?

I AM A PASTOR, AND FOR A COUPLE OF DECADES I HAVE counseled married couples. I always ask them one question: "Did you guys go through premarital counseling?" Usually, they answer with their heads down, "No, we didn't." Occasionally, they say that they had a meeting or two with their pastor or priest, but rarely were the meetings valuable. The few who had any type of formal counseling often report it was not helpful.

Because of negative experiences or a lack of experience, most men have an aversion to counseling. Those who finally seek help may find it is too late to save the marriage.[1] I would like to persuade you to pursue counseling before you get married, as you begin your marriage, or even if you have been married for several decades. But first let me try to remove the excuses that keep you from counseling.

Appendix B

"WE HAVE FRIENDS AND MENTORS; WHO NEEDS A COUNSELOR?"

A few years ago, I went to a specialist because of gastrointestinal issues. Dr. Walters (not his real name) didn't have a patient-friendly manner. I needed someone who exhibited a bit of human compassion. His personality was so off-putting that I discounted his treatment plan. I talked to friends and other people I respect, and they gave me suggestions, herbs, and supplements, which was thoughtful but didn't bring healing. Eventually, I found another doctor, and he suggested the same treatment plan as the first doctor. I followed the professional's advice and got better. Conversations with friends and mentors can be life changing. In a friendship or even a mentoring relationship, however, you are trying to attend to the needs of both people. Friendships involve a mutual exchange of listening and sharing. In counseling, the focus is solely on you. The counselor is there for you and doesn't need to please you as friends and mentors do. Tough love from a trained professional can result in a great marriage.

"I'M NOT CRAZY! COUNSELING IS FOR CRAZY PEOPLE."

We are all a little crazy, meaning that our perception of reality is sometimes askew. And we all come from and are currently in dysfunctional families because all people are deeply flawed. There are obviously spectra with regard to mental illness.[2] We might not have clinical mental illness, but we act crazy from time to time. A saying that has mistakenly been attributed to Albert Einstein is this: "Insanity is doing something over and over again and expecting a different result." Although Einstein didn't say it, the wisdom is there. I was crazy to believe that I could blow off a doctor, consult the Internet and my friends, and try to heal my own gut. We are crazy if we think we can fix our marriages on our own when we have been trying and failing.

This leads to the next myth.

"WE CAN FIGURE IT OUT"

A curse of being a successful person is that you are competent in many areas. This was one of my biggest obstacles to being counseled by a professional. When I was growing up, my motto was, "If it is going to be, it is up to me." Especially after my dad left my mom, I had to figure out how to be a man on my own. I couldn't rely on anyone other than myself to learn about finances, business, and athletics. Sure, I sought out mentors, but I prided myself on making it happen in my own strength.

I talked to a friend at least five times about how his marriage was less than satisfying. Every single time he complained about his marriage, I suggested a counselor friend of mine. And to every suggestion, he replied, "I think we can work through it." After a couple of years of trying to fix his marriage in his own strength, he ran out of resources. He went to a counselor by himself and admitted that his motto of "I got this" had destroyed his wife's trust. Eventually, my friend's wife joined him with the counselor for multiple sessions. Today this couple has one of the best marriages I have seen. A little humility goes a long way for marriages that improve.

"IT'S TOO EXPENSIVE"

Counseling costs money. My wife and I entered counseling just after the worst economic downturn for the United States since the Great Depression. We had just had our fourth child and needed a bigger house. Because of the downturn, Amie and I lost half of what we had invested in the stock market. After praying and asking, "God, what should I do?" I sensed him saying in my heart, *Invest in your family; you'll always get a good return.* Investing in counseling fit into my portfolio. We invest in what we believe is going to give us a good return. Not going to counseling because you fear the cost reveals that you don't really believe your marriage is worth greatness.

"I DON'T WANT TO BE GANGED UP ON"

Another friend summoned up the courage and the cash and freed his schedule to see a counselor with his wife. His wife had been going to the counselor on and off for years. Starting in session one, it was my friend against his wife and the counselor. Every session was an emotional beating. Throughout the years I have heard this story a few times from various people. A major obstacle to seeking counseling for some people is that they have already been there.

This friend's experience is rare in my memory of these experiences. He was tempted to chuck the whole thing, now having a great excuse. Instead of giving up, though, he found a new counselor who was more neutral, and his marriage is on the mend. A good counselor is going to challenge you, not hammer you. You can find one if you persevere. Usually it takes three to five meetings to discern if it's a good fit. I know several counselors who will see only the couple together to avoid favoritism. That can be a wise approach.

"I'M AFRAID MY PERSONAL ISSUES WILL LEAK OUT"

Quite honestly, this was a big concern for me. I lead a large church and work with possibly the most influential organization in our city, the St. Louis Cardinals. What would happen if my issues become fodder for conversations for friends, strangers, coworkers, and God forbid, the media? Privacy is a valid issue, but recognize that professional counselors must abide by strict ethical standards. They are bound ethically and legally not to discuss with others anything you tell them. Nevertheless, a counselor would be obligated legally to discuss the details of a client's sessions for a few reasons:

1. If the client has communicated a serious threat of physical violence toward him- or herself or someone else.
2. If the counselor has reasonable cause to believe that the client is so unable to care for him- or herself that the situation is life threatening.
3. If there is any child abuse or elder abuse.[3]

Your secrets are safe with your counselor.

"I WON'T KNOW WHAT TO SAY"

The bad news about counseling is that you are not in control. For some people, this obstacle is almost insurmountable. But the good news about counseling is that you are not in control. You don't have to come up with all the questions, and you certainly don't have to know all the answers. In my personal experience, these aspects are quite freeing.

Your counselor is more than capable of flying the conversation plane. Good counselors ask good questions. Good counselors will discern through your mood, questions, and answers where to take the conversation for the good of your marriage.

The first few times I went to counseling, I tried to think up how to use my questions and themes to control the session. Doing this resulted in wasting time and money and my getting shushed by the counselor. Finally, I relaxed, trusted the process, and let the counselor be the pilot.

"IF WE TALK ABOUT OUR PROBLEMS, THEY WILL GET WORSE"

Talking about pain can produce more pain. We have all seen this in our families, relationships, and jobs. Unless you want to settle for a shallow, unsatisfying marriage, you have to go toward pain, not away from it. Discussing something painful with our spouses in the presence of a caring professional helps relieve the emotional pressure caused by being dishonest about what we truly feel. Counseling can show us a path of self-understanding. It can help us discern who we are really and interact with how our spouses experience us. In counseling, we become aware of who we are and who we can be. Our words reveal these things and, under the guidance of a counselor, can lead to marriage enrichment.

"I'M NOT SURE I CAN CHANGE"

Ah, now we see the real issue. It was mine, and it probably is yours. Tim Keller, author of *The Reason for God*, described three challenges that people face when considering Christianity. The first is content: They don't have enough information. They don't know the story of the Bible. The second is coherence: they know the story, but they can't make intellectual and emotional sense of it. The third is cost: they know and understand the story, but they don't want to give up control of their lives. An additional reason is that many of us don't want to submit to counseling. It is the personal cost, not the financial cost. We have to be willing to change and alter how we have been living our lives, which bleeds into how we have been doing marriage.

Calculating exactly how many people seek professional counseling each year is difficult. However, the American Association for Marriage and Family Therapy (AAMFT), a network of more than 50,000 therapists, sees 6.1 million people annually. Of that number, 752,370 are couples.[4]

I don't even know how many people I have guided toward professional counseling. Indirectly, the number has to be in the thousands because as I speak to thousands of people weekly, I sprinkle in challenges to seek counseling. Directly, the number has to be several hundred through pastoral counseling. After all these referrals, you would think that I would have been ready to go to counseling when my wife made the suggestion. Not so much. After all, Amie and I are the ones doing the counseling ("We can figure it out"). We had our struggles, but not like other couples ("Counseling is for crazy people"). Besides, we just had our fourth kid and money was tight ("It's too expensive"), and it will mess up what we have ("If we talk about our problems, they will get worse").

Finally, I went. It has been the best decision I have ever made. Amie appreciated my taking the lead with our marriage. We have filled many gaps in our marriage with trust. We are doing much better at believing the best about each other so that we can wade through the worst with each other. Going to counseling didn't save our marriage; it improved it dramatically. But we had to take the uncomfortable step to admit we needed help. We had to make it a priority in our schedules and invest financially in our marriage. You can do the same.

APPENDIX C

WHAT IF MY WIFE IS MORE SPIRITUAL THAN I AM?

WOMEN TEND TO BE MORE SPIRITUALLY SENSITIVE AND mature than most men. This statement might sound as if I accept stereotypes, but consider the following research:

Women make up 60 percent of American congregations. Gallup and Pew Research Center data provide these percentages for women's activities that are higher than men's: [1]

More likely to pray daily	+17 PERCENT
Read the Bible weekly	+14 PERCENT
Attend worship weekly	+10 PERCENT
Participate in a Bible study group	+8 PERCENT
Pay attention to God when making decisions	+16 PERCENT[2]

A couple of years ago I was having coffee with a friend. He and his wife had just gotten pregnant with their first child, and they were in freak-out mode. My friend was consumed with getting all his life insurance, stock investments, and career path lined out. His wife was obsessing over all things nesting—getting the nursery right, making the house baby-friendly, and planting flowers near the porch. She was also on her husband's case about his lack of interest in spiritual matters. "Why am I the one looking for a church for our family? Why am I the one who always initiates spiritual conversation?" she often asked.

That day I encouraged my friend to hear his wife's requests as desires for him as much as demands from him. Many wives want to trust their husbands with spiritual realities. They want to know that their men are not just passive observers but active responders in matters of faith.

In my twenty-five years of counseling and coaching men, I have realized that some of us don't know how to make up the gap between where we are and where our wives are spiritually. Many husbands settle for sitting in the backseat and letting their wives do all the spiritual heavy lifting. Whether you are ignorant or lazy or both, I want to challenge you not just to catch up with your wife but to be an example and take the lead in setting the spiritual climate of your marriage. Here are some things I told my friend that day:

BE A LEADER WHO SERVES

Some husbands falsely believe that *leadership* is another word for *dictatorship*. For men like this, *leadership* becomes code for intolerance that devolves into a form of control, which stunts the growth of your wife and violates her spiritual exploration.

The Bible describes marriage as a covenant, and the husband is the head (the accountable one) in regard to the terms of that covenant. This headship is to be expressed in relationship and comparison to Christ's love for us. Jesus wasn't a dictator; he was a servant. He didn't expect us to find God on our own; he came to this world and showed us who God is. Jesus didn't wait for us to clean ourselves up; he died for our sin. Jesus wasn't passive; he was active. He was a leader who served. Domineering leadership and passive support are not options. Servant leadership is the fruit of a husband who is maturing spiritually, imitating the Savior of the world.

STOP TRYING AND START TRAINING

How many times have you tried to lose weight? I have tried dozens of times. It seems that every year I summon my willpower to drop ten or fifteen pounds. My big problem is that I try. We keep trying because we love shortcuts. Shortcuts are low-cost strategies for getting what we want. As I said in *The Dude's Guide to Manhood*,

> Accomplishing anything of significance doesn't happen because we try really hard but because we train really well. We can try a new restaurant or try a different wardrobe. We can even try a better diet. But we can't just try to get our waistlines back to high school proportions. We can't just try to bench-press three hundred pounds.
>
> You can't mature spiritually by trying hard, but

> training well. The companion of trying is will-power. The companion of training is discipline. Discipline is doing what you don't want to do, so that you are free to do what you do want to do. . . .
>
> Discipline temporarily constrains and constricts us for the purpose of making available a greater good. When we are disciplined, we say no to more immediate pleasures, but yes to long-term fulfillment. Discipline limits us for a season in order to deepen our ability to enjoy the world and develop the character and skills within us that we need to flourish.

Growing spiritually involves a lifetime of discipline that strengthens your heart, your affections, and your resolve to love God with all your heart, soul, mind, and strength and to love your neighbor as yourself. The word *neighbor* means "one who is near." And who is nearer than your wife?

PICK YOUR SPOTS

Too many husbands believe the myth that they need to have their spiritual act together in every way at all times. Yes, there are certain places and arenas in which you can exercise spiritual strength. Grabbing your wife's hand and praying a simple prayer before going to bed can be huge. Taking the initiative to get your kids ready for worship services is another. But you don't have to be a spiritual superman. You just have to be sensitive to and obedient to the Spirit.

APPENDIX D

WHAT ARE THE LOVE LANGUAGES?

AS INTRODUCED IN CHAPTER 7, "SERVE," THE LOVE-languages concept is the synthesis of what Dr. Gary Chapman saw in couples over years of relationship counseling. He asked each spouse what he or she desired in order to be loved. It became clear that what made one spouse feel loved did not necessarily make the other one feel loved. He boiled these responses down to five primary love languages: acts of service, physical touch, quality time, words of affirmation, and receiving gifts.

Learning each other's love language is a practical way to pursue your wife and to cultivate romance and passion in your marriage every day. It's not always sexy or exciting, but the impact over time is big. Learning to love each other through love languages is a way to stay in love over a lifetime of marriage.

Your wife may intuitively know her love language, or you may have to do some work to find out what feels like love to her (or doesn't). This is easier when you have the same love language and more challenging when you don't. No one love language is superior to another; all are valid whether or not you understand or relate to them.

Here are practical ways for you to demonstrate love to your wife in her language:

DO ACTS OF SERVICE

Your wife will feel pursued and loved when you take time and energy to serve her in practical ways, both large and small.

Consider these suggestions:

- Fill her car with gas, or check the oil and air up the tires.
- Clean out her car for her and wash it.
- Take ongoing responsibility for tasks that she dislikes.
- Find out what feels like service to her, and do those things (washing dishes, helping with kids' baths, running errands, cooking, laundering clothes, and so on).
- Make yourself available to help, particularly during stressful times (holidays, visits by house guests, crises, or transitions such as moving, starting a new job, and beginning the school year).

- Don't assume that what feels helpful to you also feels helpful to her. Ask her.
- Give your wife the freedom to ask you for help by responding with a positive attitude and following through on what you say you will do.

USE PHYSICAL TOUCH

Your wife will feel pursued and loved when you touch her often, intentionally and affectionately.

Consider these suggestions:

- Touch your wife often in affectionate ways.
- Give her a foot, hand, or back massage without being asked and without having a time limit.
- Hold your wife's hand, or put your arm around her in private and in public.
- Check in with her physically (squeeze her hand, give her a quick kiss, stand close to her) at events where you're socializing with others.
- Greet and leave her with a physically affectionate gesture.

SPEND QUALITY TIME

Your wife will feel pursued and loved when you spend regular and intentional time with her and give her your undivided attention.

Consider these suggestions:

- Set boundaries for yourself with your phone, computer, TV, video games, or anything else that is a consistent distraction.
- Take responsibility for regular times when you are alone with your wife and she has your undivided attention.
- Stay engaged in whatever activity you have chosen to do together, whether it is watching a movie or working in the yard.
- Do a time inventory to find out where you spend your time and where you can make changes that will allow you to spend more time with your wife.
- Look at your wife when she's talking to you. Sit down with her when she wants to talk to you. Teach your children when and how to interrupt appropriately.
- Take responsibility for planning dates, getaways, or vacations for you and your wife. Manage at least some of the logistics (travel details, budget, child care arrangements) so that your wife isn't overly burdened by those details.
- Initiate activities that you and your wife enjoy and can do together consistently (eating out; going to movies, concerts, or sports events; doing exercise).
- Try new things together. You don't have to do them again if you don't enjoy them, but you might find something new that's fun.

CHOOSE WORDS OF AFFIRMATION

Your wife will feel pursued and loved when you genuinely and thoughtfully affirm and encourage her on a regular basis.

Consider these suggestions:

- Ask your wife what feels and doesn't feel affirming to her (word choice, tone, topic).
- Leave your wife thank-you notes for things that she does for you on a regular basis. Leave the notes in places related to the compliment (coffee maker, laundry room).
- Make mental and physical notes of things that you appreciate about your wife, and think through how to affirm her in ways that will be meaningful to her.
- Send encouraging texts or e-mails.
- Praise your wife genuinely to other people and in front of other people, including your children.
- Tell other people about areas where your wife excels.

GIVE GIFTS

Your wife will feel pursued and loved when you give her thoughtfully chosen gifts on a regular basis.

Consider these suggestions:

- Keep a running list of things that your wife likes, as well as clothing, shoe, and jewelry sizes.
- Make notes of items that she mentions that she would

enjoy having, marks in a magazine, or sees on a website. Remember types of flowers, particular brands or stores, and gum, candy, snack, and music preferences.

- Surprise her with small gifts in unexpected places (glove box, refrigerator drawer, under her pillow).
- Include a budget category for regular and consistent gifts for your wife.
- Plan ahead for larger or more involved gifts. Subscribe to e-mail lists for brands or stores that she likes so that you can take advantage of sales or promotions.
- Get help if needed to wrap gifts in an attractive or creative way. It matters.
- Keep a stash of gift cards to stores that she enjoys. They don't have to be for large amounts.
- Ask her close friends or relatives for gift ideas.
- Make a big deal out of her birthday, your anniversary, and Mother's Day.

Husband, you need to apply the same passion to pursuing your wife according to her love language that you do to your job or favorite hobby. Learning to speak your wife's love language requires trial and error. Don't give up if she doesn't immediately respond with overflowing gratitude.

The goal is for the pursuit of your wife according to her love language to become an ongoing habit. Like the forming of any habit, it takes your time, commitment, and discipline on an ongoing basis. You will have to make adjustments over time, assess your progress, and reestablish these habits when you get offtrack.

NOTES

CHAPTER 1: LISTEN

1. A few years ago, a statistic was floating around that men speak an average of seven thousand words a day, while women speak an average of twenty thousand words a day. When I first heard those numbers, my marriage struggles suddenly had context. Though it rings true for many of us, the notion was debunked. It originally received prominent attention in Louann Brizendine's *The Female Brain* (New York: Broadway Books, 2006). But according to Matthias Mehl, researcher at the University of Arizona, "no one had ever systematically recorded the total daily output in natural conversations of a sizable number of people." Richard Knox, "Study: Men Talk Just as Much as Women Do," NPR.org, July 5, 2007, http://www.npr.org/templates/story/story.php?storyId=11762186).
2. Deborah Tannen, *You Just Don't Understand: Women and Men in Conversation* (New York: HarperCollins, 1990) 24–25.
3. "Accustomed to working through emotional problems with her female friends, the wife is likely to find her husband's withdrawal devastating, infuriating, and inexplicable." John Gottman, *Why Marriages Succeed or Fail* (New York: Simon & Schuster, 1994), 148.
4. John Gottman, *The Seven Principles for Making Marriage Work* (New York: Three Rivers Press, 1999), 88–89. Sue Johnson wrote, "If I appeal to you for emotional connection and you respond intellectually to a problem, rather than directly to me, on an attachment level I will experience that as 'no response.' This is one of the reasons that the research on social support uniformly states that people want 'indirect' support, that is, emotional confirmation and caring from their partners, rather than advice." The tragedy here is that a man may be doing his best to answer his wife's concerns by offering advice and solutions, not understanding that what she is really seeking from him is emotional engagement. His engagement is the solution for her. *Hold Me Tight* (New York: Little, Brown and Company, 2008), 83.
5. This is one implication of Paul Ekman's work on smiles. Mark G. Frank and Paul Ekman, "Physiological Effects of the Smile," *Directions in Psychiatry* 16 (December 10, 1996), https://www.paulekman.com/wp-content/uploads/2013/07/Physiological-Effects-Of-The-Smile.pdf.

6. Gary Smalley, *Secrets to Lasting Love* (New York: Fireside, 2000), 166–201.
7. John and Stasi Eldredge, *Captivating* (Nashville: Thomas Nelson, 2010), 42.

CHAPTER 3: FIGHT

1. How your family of origin impacts your marriage: According to Dr. Sue Johnson, "Love relationships are not rational bargains, they are emotional bonds. Similar to the bond between a mother and a child. The way we attach as adult lovers tends to reflect the way we attached as children to our primary caregivers."
2. Temperament and personality, as concepts in the social sciences, tend to have fluid definitions. There are various opinions on the matter in contemporary scholarship. But for the sake of consistency and your conflict, you can understand temperament as the innate characteristics and aspects of personality. To put it another way, personality (behaviors, feelings, thoughts) is built upon temperament. "What Is Temperament?" in *Psychology Dictionary*, http://psychologydictionary.org/temperament/.
3. Our temptation is to give ourselves too much credit for our innate strengths and others too much criticism for their innate weaknesses. Despite that, we can increase our awareness and accommodation of other personality styles. We don't get a pass when it comes to our blind spots. We *can* develop the strengths inherent to our personalities and control/manage our weaknesses.
4. This is the best *free* personality test online: www.humanmetrics.com/cgi-win/JTypes1.htm. Once you find out your type, you can read the full description here: www.humanmetrics.com/cgi-win/JungType.htm.
5. Sue Johnson, *Hold Me Tight* (New York: Little, Brown and Company, 2008), 66–67.
6. With various definitions of temperament and personality being employed in scholarship, it is easy to find articles that reject the permanence of personality. In the late 1980s, Dr. Paul Costa and Robert McCrae, psychologists at the National Institute on Aging in Baltimore, interviewed thousands of people throughout the United States in 1975 and in 1984. It was one of the largest studies ever performed on the topic. Costa and McCrae concluded that three basic aspects of personality change little, if at all, over the course of someone's life: *a person's anxiety level*, *friendliness*, and *eagerness for novel experiences*. On the other hand, traits such as alienation, morale, and feelings of satisfaction can vary greatly throughout one's life. Daniel Goleman, "Personality," *New York Times*, June 9, 1987, http://www.nytimes.com/1987/06/09/science/personality-major-traits-found-stable-through-life.html.
7. Bradford Health Services, "HALT: The Dangers of Hunger, Anger, Loneliness, and Tiredness," accessed July 16, 2015, http://bradfordhealth.com/halt-hunger-anger-loneliness-tiredness.
8. "When one partner makes a complaint, the other repeats it back in [his or her] own words, trying to capture not just the thought, but also the feelings that go with it. The partner mirroring checks with the other to be sure the restatement is on target, and if not, tries again until it is right—something that seems simple, but is surprisingly tricky in execution. The effect of being mirrored accurately is not just feeling understood, but having the added sense of being in emotional attunement." Daniel Goleman, *Emotional Intelligence* (New York: Bantam, 2006), 146.

CHAPTER 4: GROW

1. David Snowdon, *Aging With Grace: What the Nun Study Teaches Us About Leading Longer, Healthier, and More Meaningful Lives* (New York: Bantam, 2002). Sue Halpen, "Can't Remember What I Forgot, Brain Exercises: Do They Work," *Psychology Today*, August 29, 2008, http://www.psychologytoday.com/blog/cant-remember-what-i-forgot/200808/brain-exercises-do-they-work-chapter-1.
2. Caroline Carpenter, "Reading Agency Survey Finds 63% of Men Rarely Read,"

Bookseller.com, April 16, 2014, www.thebookseller.com/news/reading-agency-survey-finds-63-men-rarely-read.html.
3. American Counseling Association, "2014 ACA Code of Ethics," accessed June 22, 2015, http://www.counseling.org/resources/aca-code-of-ethics.pdf.
4. *Merriam-Webster*, s.v. "affinity," www.merriam-webster.com/dictionary/affinity.
5. For more on the difference between friendship and affinity, read chapter 8, "The Connected Man," from my book, *The Dude's Guide to Manhood* (Nashville: Thomas Nelson, 2014), 99–113.
6. Ibid.
7. Cited in Sue Johnson, *Love Sense* (New York: Little, Brown and Company, 2013), 73.
8. Ibid., 70.
9. Ibid.
10. Gary Thomas, *Sacred Pathways* (Grand Rapids, MI: Zondervan, 2000).
11. Tim Keller, *The Reason for God* (New York: Dutton, 2008), chapter 1, "There Can't Be Just *One* True Religion"; Lee Strobel, *The Case for Christ* (Grand Rapids, MI: Zondervan, 2000); John 14:6; Acts 4:12.

CHAPTER 5: PROVIDE

1. Michael Kimmel, *Guyland* (New York: HarperCollins, 2008), 24.
2. John Ortberg defines *discipline* as "any activity I can do by direct effort that will help me do what I cannot now do by direct effort." Cited in Darrin Patrick, *The Dude's Guide to Manhood* (Nashville: Thomas Nelson, 2014), 35. For more on discipline, refer to chapter 3, "Train, Don't Just Try," from *The Dude's Guide to Manhood.*
3. According to 2012 census figures, from 1980 to 2008, the percentage of all births to unmarried women rose from 18.4 percent to 40.6 percent. The percentage of single-parent households went from 19.5 percent to 29.5 percent (an increase of four million households). United States Census Bureau, www.census.gov/compendia/statab/2012/tables/12s1337.pdf.
4. East St. Louis tops the list, but it's not as if the rest of St. Louis is in the clear, coming in at number 12. Neighborhood Scout's Most Dangerous Cities, 2015, www.neighborhoodscout.com/neighborhoods/crime-rates/top100dangerous/.
5. Sarah Knapton, "Working Mothers Trapped by 'Double Burden' of Guilt," *Telegraph* (UK), February 19, 2014, www.telegraph.co.uk/science/science-news/10648965/Working-mothers-trapped-by-double-burden-of-guilt.html.
6. "The History of Work," *Reader's Digest*, www.readersdigest.com.au/history-of-work.
7. Kay Hymowitz, *Manning Up: How the Rise of Women Has Turned Men into Boys* (New York: Basic Books, 2012); Hanna Rosin, *The End of Men: And the Rise of Women* (New York: Riverhead Books, 2012); Camille Paglia, "It's a Man's World, and It Always Will Be," *Time*, December, 16. 2013, ideas.time.com/2013/12/16/its-a-mans-world-and-it-always-will-be/.
8. Patrick, *Dude's Guide to Manhood*, 43.
9. Ibid., 78.
10. Brittany Ruess, "A Look Inside Urban Farming Efforts in St. Louis and Kansas City," *Missouri Times*, http://themissouritimes.com/7355/look-inside-urban-farming-efforts-st-louis-kansas-city/.
11. Andy Crouch, *Culture Making* (Downers Grove, IL: InterVarsity, 2008), 107.
12. Ibid., 114.
13. Romans 5:12–14; 1 Timothy 2:14–15.
14. Sociologist Bradford Wilcox argues that the notion that contemporary women are looking for husbands to be fathers "who will split their time evenly between work and family life" is a myth. "It may be true for the average journalist or academic, but it is not true for the average American married mom." Bradford Wilcox, "Five Myths on Fathers and Family," Love and Fidelity Network.org., http://www.loveandfidelity.org/online

_journal/five-myths-on-fathers-and-family-by-dr-bradford-wilcox/. A 2007 Pew Research Center study found that only 21 percent of mothers with children under eighteen wanted to work full-time, compared with 72 percent of fathers with children under eighteen. Pew Research Center, "Fewer Mothers Prefer Full-time Work," July 12, 2007, www.pewsocialtrends.org/2007/07/12/fewer-mothers-prefer-full-time-work/.

15. John Piper wrote, "This is implied in Genesis 3 where the curse touches man and woman in their natural places of life. It is not a curse that man must work in the field to get bread for the family or that woman bears children. The curse is that these spheres of life are made difficult and frustrating. In appointing the curse for his rebellious creatures God aims at the natural sphere of life peculiar to each." John Piper and Wayne Grudem, eds., *Recovering Biblical Manhood and Womanhood* (Wheaton, IL: Crossway, 2006), 35.
16. Sandra Richter, *Epic of Eden* (Downers Grove, IL: InterVarsity, 2008), 111.
17. Patrick, *Dude's Guide to Manhood*, 45.

CHAPTER 6: REST

1. Juliet Schor, *The Overworked American: The Unexpected Decline of Leisure* (New York: Basic Books, 1992).
2. American Psychological Association, *By the Numbers: A Psychologically Healthy Workplace Fact Sheet*, November 20, 2013, www.apaexcellence.org/resources/goodcompany/newsletter/article/487.
3. Rebecca Ray, Milla Sanes, and John Schmitt, "No-Vacation Nation Revisited," Center for Economic and Policy Research, May 2013, www.cepr.net/index.php/publications/reports/no-vacation-nation-2013.
4. Carolyn Gregoire, "These Countries Are So Much Better Than America When It Comes to Work-Life Balance," *Huffington Post*, April 11, 2014; On tax rates, see Steven Landsburg, "Why Europeans Work Less Than Americans," *Forbes*, May 23, 2006.
5. "God saw everything that he had made, and behold, it was very good" (Gen. 1:31).
6. New York University sociologist Dalton Conley is reported to have coined the term. Thom Patterson, "Welcome to the 'Weisure' Lifestyle," CNN, May 11, 2009, www.cnn.com/2009/LIVING/worklife/05/11/weisure/.
7. "Waiting on the Lord" is one of the most important exhortations in the Bible. In the Psalms, it is both a command and a declaration of hope that God will bring about good for his people in due time (Pss. 27:14; 62:1–12; 130:5–8; 145:15). Ecclesiastes 3:11 tells us that God "has made everything beautiful in its time," suggesting that his sovereign plan is never compromised, even though we cannot explain how particular circumstances fit into that larger picture. Hence the last half of the verse: "Also, he has put eternity into man's heart, yet so that he cannot find out what God has done from the beginning to the end."
8. John Ortberg, *The Life You've Always Wanted*, expanded edition (Grand Rapids, MI: Zondervan, 2002), 76–77.
9. Tony Schwartz, "Relax! You'll Be More Productive," *New York Times*, February 9, 2013, www.nytimes.com/2013/02/10/opinion/sunday/relax-youll-be-more-productive.html?pagewanted=all. It references the 2007 *Journal of Occupational and Environmental Medicine* report on absenteeism and "presenteeism" (days the employee was at work but performing at less than full capacity because of health reasons) found in "Fatigue in the Workplace Is Common and Costly," *Medical News Today*, January 15, 2007, www.medicalnewstoday.com/releases/60732.php.
10. Sandra Richter, *Epic of Eden* (Downers Grove, IL: InterVarsity, 2008), 104–5.
11. Ibid., 105.
12. Mark Buchanan, *The Rest of God* (Nashville: Thomas Nelson, 2006), 3.
13. Charles R. Swindoll, *Growing Strong in the Seasons of Life* (Grand Rapids, MI: Zondervan, 1983), 354.

14. Wayne Muller, *Sabbath: Finding Rest, Renewal, and Delight in Our Busy Lives* (New York: Bantam, 1999), 31.
15. Hebrews 13:4.
16. Kathleen Berchelmann, "Tired? What Sleep Deprivation Does to Parents," ChildrensMD.org, May 6, 2013, http://childrensmd.org/browse-by-age-group/pregnancy-childbirth/tired-what-sleep-deprivation-does-to-parents/.

CHAPTER 7: SERVE

1. Gary Chapman, *The Five Love Languages* (Chicago: Northfield Publishing, 1992).
2. Ibid.
3. The American Institute of Stress, "What Is Stress?," accessed June 22, 2015, www.stress.org/what-is-stress.
4. Stress Management Society, "What Is Stress?," accessed June 22, 2015, www.stress.org.uk/What-is-stress.aspx; National Institute of Mental Health, "Q&A on Stress for Adults: How It Affects Your Health and What You Can Do About It," accessed June 22, 2015, www.nimh.nih.gov/health/publications/stress/index.shtml.
5. Akihito Shimazu, Arnold B. Bakker, and Evangelia Demerouti, "How Job Demands Affect an Intimate Partner," *Journal of Occupational Health* 51 (2009): 239–48, www.beanmanaged.eu/pdf/articles/arnoldbakker/article_arnold_bakker_192.pdf; Cory Williams, "Marital Satisfaction and Job Satisfaction," Examiner.com, April 13, 2011, www.examiner.com/article/marital-satisfaction-and-job-satisfaction-there-is-a-connection.
6. A landmark ten-year study done by UCLA's Sloan Center on Everyday Lives of Families has shown that women more than men need to be in a clutter-free environment in order to relax. Cited in Farnoosh Torabi's *When She Makes More: 10 Rules for Breadwinning Women* (New York: Hudson Street Press, 2014), 126.
7. "How Career Women Still Do Most of the Chores . . . Even When They're the Main Breadwinner," *Daily Mail* (UK), July 21, 2013, www.dailymail.co.uk/news/article-2372772/Career-women-chores-theyre-main-breadwinner.html. Torabi commented, "Although the study, done by Britain's Economic and Social Research Council (ESRC), looked at European households, my guess is the numbers would reflect other households in developed nations, the United States included." *When She Makes More: 10 Rules for Breadwinning Women,* 234.
8. Carin Rubenstein, *The Superior Wife Syndrome* (New York: Touchstone, 2009), 130–31.
9. Ibid., 75–76.

CHAPTER 8: SUBMIT

1. C. S. Lewis, *Mere Christianity* (New York: HarperCollins, 1980), 122.
2. Phil Jackson quoted in "The Soul of Teamwork," Dailygood.org, May 13, 2013, www.dailygood.org/story/430/the-soul-of-teamwork-phil-jackson-in-an-interview-by-ross-robertson/.
3. Ibid.
4. Mary Kassian, "7 Misconceptions about Submission," Girlsgonewise.com, November 15, 2011, www.girlsgonewise.com/7-misconceptions-about-submission/.

CHAPTER 9: PURSUE

1. Darrin Patrick, *The Dude's Guide to Manhood* (Nashville: Thomas Nelson, 2014), chapter 6, "Love a Woman: Become a Devoted Man," 73–86.
2. Kevin Leman, *Sheet Music: Uncovering the Secrets of Sexual Intimacy in Marriage* (Carol Stream, IL: Tyndale House, 2003).

CHAPTER 10: WORSHIP

1. Anthony Hoekema, *Created In God's Image* (Grand Rapids, MI: Eerdmans, 1986), 67–68.
2. Ibid.

3. John Piper, *God's Passion for His Glory: Living the Vision of Jonathan Edwards* (Wheaton IL: Crossway, 2006). Piper's work contains the highly influential dissertation from Edwards, *The End for Which God Created the World*.
4. This is the central thesis of John Piper's *Desiring God* (Colorado Springs: Multnomah, 2011).
5. This illustration is commonly attributed to Charles Spurgeon.
6. Tim Keller wrote, "Luther saw how the Old Testament law against idols and the New Testament emphasis on justification by faith alone are essentially the same. He said that the Ten Commandments begin with two commandments against idolatry. It is because the fundamental problem in law-breaking is always idolatry. In other words, we never break the other commandments without first breaking the law against idolatry. Luther understood that the first commandment is really all about justification by faith, and to fail to believe in justification by faith is idolatry, which is the root of all that displeases God." Tim Keller, "Talking About Idolatry in a Postmodern Age," cited in Tim Brister, "Keller, Luther, and How the Law Exposes Functional Idolatry," TimmyBrister.com, February 29, 2013.
7. Darrin Patrick, *Church Planter: The Man, The Message, The Mission* (Wheaton, IL: Crossway, 2010), 137.
8. "In the Bible there is no more serious charge than that of idolatry. Idolatry called for the strictest punishment, elicited the most disdainful polemic, prompted the most extreme measure of avoidance, and was regarded as the chief identifying characteristic of those who were the very antithesis of the people of God." Brian S. Rosner, "Idolatry," in *New Dictionary of Biblical Theology: Exploring the Unity and Diversity of Scripture*, eds. T. Desmond Alexander, Brian S. Rosner, D. A. Carson, and Graeme Goldsworthy (Downers Grove, IL: InterVarsity, 2000), 570.

APPENDIX B: WHAT IF I'M SCARED OF COUNSELING?

1. This is one of the major reasons why some people have concluded that marriage counseling is ineffective. Erica Manfred, "Why Marriage Counseling Doesn't Work," *Huffington Post*, May 16, 2011, www.huffingtonpost.com/erica-manfred/why-marriage-counseling-d_b_860493.html.
2. Clinicians use this source to classify mental disorders: *Diagnostic and Statistical Manual of Mental Disorders* (DSM-V), 5th ed. (Arlington, VA: American Psychiatric Association Publishing, 2013).
3. American Counseling Association, "2014 ACA Code of Ethics," accessed July 29, 2015, http://www.counseling.org/resources/aca-code-of-ethics.pdf.
4. American Association for Marriage and Family Therapists, "AAMFT Therapy Topics," www.aamft.org/iMIS15/AAMFT/Content/Consumer_Updates/Marriage_and_Family_Therapists.aspx.

APPENDIX C: WHAT IF MY WIFE IS MORE SPIRITUAL THAN I AM?

1. National Congregations Study, Table 1, under "Social Composition," 11, accessed June 22, 2015, www.soc.duke.edu/natcong/Docs/SummaryTables.pdf.
2. Albert Winseman, "Religion and Gender: A Congregation Divided," Gallup.com, December 3, 2002, www.gallup.com/poll/7336/Religion-Gender-Congregation-Divided.aspx; Read Bible weekly (W-43% M-29%); Participate in a Bible study group (W-18% M-10%); Decisions: pay attention to God (W-56% M-40%); Decisions: pay attention to own views (W-37% M-54%). *U.S. Religious Landscape Survey* (conducted in 2007); Pew Research Center, "The Stronger Sex—Spiritually Speaking," February 26, 2009, www.pewforum.org/2009/02/26/the-stronger-sex-spiritually-speaking/. Pray at least daily (W-66% M-49%); Say religion is very important in their lives (W-63% M-49%); Have absolutely certain belief in a personal God (W-58% M-45%); Attend worship services at least weekly (W-44% M-34%).

ABOUT THE AUTHORS

DARRIN PATRICK FOUNDED THE Journey in 2002 in the urban core of Saint Louis, Missouri. The Journey has six locations and has released seven church plants. Darrin is vice president of the Acts 29 Church Planting Network and has helped start multiple nonprofits in Saint Louis. He also serves as chaplain to the Saint Louis Cardinals.

After earning his BA in biblical languages from Southwest Baptist University and a master's of divinity (summa cum laude) from Midwestern Baptist Theological Seminary, Darrin earned his doctor of ministry from Covenant Seminary. Darrin is author of *The Dude's Guide to Manhood*, *Church Planter*, coauthor of *Replant*, and *For the City*, and contributor to the *ESV Gospel Transformation Bible* and *Don't Call It a Comeback.*

Darrin is married to his high school sweetheart, Amie, and they have four beautiful children: Glory, Grace, Drew, and Delainey.

- Blog/Resources: DarrinPatrick.org
- Twitter: @DarrinPatrick
- Facebook.com/DarrinPatrick
- Instagram.com/drdarrinpatrick
- The Dude's Guide: TheDudesGuide.org

AMIE PATRICK IS A TEACHER, WRITER, and pastor's wife. Married to her high school sweetheart, Darrin, for twenty-two years, she is also the proud mom of four great kids. Amie holds a degree in music education and is passionate about leadership, the arts, teaching women to practically apply the gospel to all areas of their lives, and helping pastors and church planters' wives thrive in their calling.

- Twitter: @AmiePatrick